Incorporating
the
Professional Practice

Incorporating the Professional Practice

George E. Ray

Prentice-Hall, Inc.
Englewood Cliffs, N.J.

PRENTICE-HALL INTERNATIONAL, INC., *London*
PRENTICE-HALL OF AUSTRALIA, PTY. LTD., *Sydney*
PRENTICE-HALL OF CANADA, LTD., *Toronto*
PRENTICE-HALL OF INDIA PRIVATE LTD., *New Delhi*
PRENTICE-HALL OF JAPAN, INC., *Tokyo*

LIBRARY OF CONGRESS
CATALOG CARD NUMBER: 70–180597

PRINTED IN THE UNITED STATES OF AMERICA
ISBN 0–13–455915–0
B & P

ABOUT THE AUTHOR

George E. Ray, a partner in the Dallas, Texas law firm of McCulloch, Ray, Trotti & Hemphill, has devoted his 36 years of practice largely to matters related to taxation. He served as attorney for the United States Board of Tax Appeals, now the United States Tax Court, as a Special Assistant to the Attorney General in the Tax Division of the Department of Justice and as principal attorney in the Office of the Tax Legislative Counsel of the Treasury Department. He has lectured extensively on tax and estate planning matters at Southern Methodist University Law School, the Southwestern Legal Foundation, The Practising Law Institute and institutes sponsored by New York University, The University of Southern California, The University of Michigan, as well as institutes sponsored by bar associations in the states of Georgia, Missouri and Colorado, as well as Texas. He is the author of more than 60 articles in tax and legal periodicals, including a large number on the subject of professional corporations. He is the co-author of several books. The author is a graduate of Harvard College, magna cum laude, The Harvard Law School and served as a faculty tax research associate at Columbia University Law School.

How This Book Will Help
Professionals and Their Advisors

This book provides a practical and constructive approach to help the professional adopt the professional corporation as the form in which to carry on his professional practice. The book is directed to the professional and his advisors, his lawyer, accountant, life underwriter, investment advisor, actuary and trust officer, as well as the clinic or firm manager.

This is a book on survival. It is financial survival for the professional, who finds himself squeezed between the Scylla of inflation and the Charybdis of taxes. Try as hard as he will, the professional man finds himself going forward 2 feet, only to fall back 3. During the period since the 1954 Revenue Act was adopted by Congress, while tax rates have not increased, the true, effective rate of taxes has increased each year by the amount of inflation, or up to as much as 6% per year. The net result is that the true taxes which the professional man pays on his income and on his estate have virtually doubled since 1954. While the professional is now making more money in terms of dollars, he finds it harder and harder to save anything at all after paying his expenses and taxes. When he has the figures run on his estate, he finds that on his death a large portion of what he leaves will go out in the form of Federal Estate Tax.

The professional corporation enables the professional to convert his highest tax dollars, at the top of his bracket, to the protection of his family in the event of his death, and for himself when retired. It also permits him to adopt a regular system of investment and savings, as well as provide similar benefits to all his employees. It enables the professional to do some intelligent tax, estate and investment planning. It does not come free, but at least he gets a reasonably "fair shake" compared to ordinary corporate owner-employees, even though he does not get stock options, restricted stock or a chance to make capital gains on stock investments as they do.

Who should take advantage of this opportunity? Very broadly speaking, all professional people in the 30% or higher income tax bracket. All but the improvident are already spending something to protect their families and themselves by insurance and savings. They can do more, at less cost, through the use of the professional corporation.

George E. Ray

Table of Contents

Contents

Contents

Contents

Chapter 2

HOW DO YOU GO ABOUT ORGANIZING THE CORPORATION?

Contents

Contents

Chapter 3

HOW DO YOU GET PROPERTY INTO AND OUT OF THE CORPORATION?

Contents

Chapter 4

HOW DO YOU HANDLE COMPENSATION?

Contents

Chapter 5

HOW DO YOU SELECT AND INSTALL THE CORPORATION RETIREMENT PLAN?

Contents

Contents

Chapter 6

HOW IS INSURANCE USED
IN THE PROFESSIONAL CORPORATION?

Contents

Chapter 7

HOW DO YOU OPERATE THE CORPORATION?

Contents

Contents

Chapter 8

WHAT ABOUT CONGRESSIONAL LEGISLATION AND THE PROFESSIONAL CORPORATION?

Contents

Chapter 9
WHAT WILL BE THE COST OF INCORPORATING?

Contents

Incorporating

the

Professional Practice

1

Why Incorporate
the Professional Practice?

Why should a professional consider incorporation and what does he hope to gain thereby? For some 30 years, professional people have had to pay ever increasing income taxes. At the same time, they have seen that their clients and patients who work for corporations have been able to obtain considerable relief on their taxes, through pension and profit-sharing plans, as well as fringe benefits provided by their corporation. With the increasing pressure on the incomes of professional people, brought about by higher income tax rates and the decrease in the value of the dollar through inflation, the disparity in tax treatment between professional people, on the one hand, and corporate employees, on the other, has become ever more striking. As a result, more professional people, through the years, have sought to set up professional associations—and where permitted by state statute, professional corporations—to obtain for themselves some of the tax benefits accorded to corporate employees. *Now this can be done in every state.*

Just what are the purposes of a professional corporation? Why should a professional go to the trouble of forming a corporation and making himself an employee? Because a professional corporation enables a professional who forms his own corporation, by himself or with fellow members of his profession, to protect himself and his family against five basic things that can happen to him:

1. He may get sick. He can provide against that through medical and hospitalization insurance, deductible by the corporation.
2. If he is disabled, he can be protected by disability insurance, paid for by the corporation and deductible to it.
3. If he lives long enough, he will get old. He can provide for that by getting the benefits of a pension plan, which will furnish him an income for life, paid for by the corporation.
4. If he dies, his widow, his estate and his family can be protected through group term insurance, paid for by the corporation and deductible to it, but not taxable to him. In addition, his pension plan can include a pension to his widow for life, with payments for a certain period of years for his children and other dependents or beneficiaries designated by him.
5. The danger that he will lose his job or suffer other financial misfortune can be protected against through a profit-sharing or thrift plan. The contributions to the plan will be deductible by the corporation, together with voluntary contributions by him, over a period of years. He can thereby save some of the income that he is earning and provide protection against his winding up, at the end of his career, with no income and no property.

Through these five types of protection, all deductible to the corporation and free of income tax to the professional, he can, in effect, put a financial umbrella over himself and his family.

There are two basic reasons why a professional person should incorporate: first, the tax advantages of a professional corporation; second, the non-tax advantages. The particular advantages, both tax and non-tax, are numerous and real. For a particular professional person, however, these advantages must be considered in the light of his own professional practice. There may be some disadvantages that follow from professional incorporation as well, and these, both as to tax and non-tax, must also be considered before a particular professional person should make his decision as to incorporation.

Why Incorporate the Professional Practice?

A. What Are the Tax Advantages?

The tax advantages of the professional corporation are many and fall into several categories. These advantages of incorporation involve making the professional an employee of his own corporation. Many tax benefits to corporate employees are possible, although they are denied to the self-employed in partnership or sole proprietorship form.

First and foremost are the tax advantages resulting from the adoption of a pension or profit-sharing plan by the corporation.

1. Contributions to Pension and Profit-Sharing Plans Are Deductible

There is an income tax deduction to the corporation in the amount of its contributions to the pension or profit-sharing plan. If the professional person is in an individual income tax bracket of 50%, for example, then the contribution by the corporation to the pension or profit-sharing plan will save him 50 cents on each dollar on his income tax. The income that would have otherwise been taxed to him in his top bracket of 50% is, instead, channelled through the corporation to the pension or profit-sharing plan. It goes into the trust fund as a tax deduction of the corporation, rather than being taxed to the individual professional as ordinary income in his top bracket.

2. The Funds Build Up Tax-Free

A second tax advantage lies in the fact that a pension or profit-sharing trust fund is exempt from income tax and builds up tax-free. As a consequence, it can accumulate income much faster than could the professional personally, or even a corporation, subject to income tax.

There are income tax advantages to the corporate employees in the tax treatment of the distributions received by them from the pension or profit-sharing plan. With a professional corporation, the professional person himself becomes an employee of the corporation and can share in these benefits, together with the other employees of the corporation.

3. The Employees Are Not Taxed Until Distributions Are Received

The distributions from the pension or profit-sharing trust fund are not taxable to the employees until they are received. At such time, the employee may be in a lower tax bracket, and this will particularly be true if the income is received by him after he has retired.

4. Pension or Annuity Income Will Not Cost Any Retirement Income Credit

In computing the retirement income credit, a pension or annuity is not considered to be earned income. The pension or annuity will not cost the employee any of his retirement income credit. In addition, employee annuities are exempt from income tax during the first three years if the amounts received do not exceed the employee's own contributions. In other words, the employee can get back his contributions tax-free for the first three years, if they are received in the form of an annuity.

5. Capital Gain Treatment as to Some Distributions

Another tax benefit which flows to the employee arises from the fact that where the distributions from the trust fund are all made in one taxable year, then the portion which represents contributions of the employer will receive the benefit of an averaging procedure. They will be taxed at a rate which would apply to one-seventh of the total distribution and thus fall in a lower bracket. The balance of the distribution, representing income and growth, will be taxed as capital gain.

6. No Estate Tax on Survivor Benefits

In addition to the income tax advantages resulting from the pension or profit-sharing fund, there is a complete estate tax exemption on survivor benefits received under a qualified pension or profit-sharing plan, and there is no gift tax on the election of survivor benefits by the employee under the plan.

There are many other tax benefits flowing from the professional corporation which are not related to the pension or profit-sharing plan. Many of these benefits are very substantial.

7. The Employees May Receive Group Term Life Insurance Benefits Tax-Free

Corporate employees may receive the benefits of group term life insurance paid for by the corporation, tax-free to the employee.

Why Incorporate the Professional Practice?

8. The Employees May Receive Payments Tax-Free from Accident, Health and Sickness Insurance Plans

Corporate employees may receive payments tax-free from accident, health and sickness insurance plans, even though the employer has paid for the insurance with tax-deductible dollars.

9. The Employees May Receive Sick-Pay Benefits Tax-Free up to $100 per Week

Payments to employees for sickness, and in lieu of wages, are exempt from income tax to the extent that they do not exceed $100 per week.

10. Death Benefits to Employees, up to $5,000, Are Tax-Free

Death benefits to corporate employees, up to a maximum of $5,000, are exempt from all tax. In some cases, this amount may be increased if it involves the widow of a taxpayer and she can prove that it constitutes a bona fide gift, rather than compensation.

There are some tax advantages which are available to corporate employees, but which do not particularly apply to professional corporations. Among these benefits are those related to stock options, stock bonuses, restricted stock and deferred compensation plans.

The professional corporation itself, as distinguished from a partnership or sole proprietorship, has some tax advantages which may prove, in a particular case, very worthwhile.

11. Corporate 22% Rate Available

The income of the corporation may be subject to the favorable 22% rate on the first $25,000 of taxable income.

12. The 85% Dividends-Received Exclusion

The corporation may also benefit from the dividends-received deduction, which will relieve the corporation of tax on 85% of dividends received by it from other corporations. The net effect of this deduction is to reduce the effective rate of tax on the corporate income, received in the form of dividends, to 3.3% at the 22% corporate rate, or 7.2% at the corporate 48% rate of tax.

13. The Corporation Has a Free Choice to Select a Fiscal Year

A corporation, as distinguished from a partnership or proprietorship, has a completely free choice to select a fiscal year; whereas, partnerships formed after 1954 are limited to the same taxable year as the partners themselves.

Adding up all of these tax benefits, some pertaining to corporate employees and some to the corporation itself, makes it clear that a professional corporation, by virtue of its corporate tax status, can bring a very considerable number of tax benefits to the corporation and its employees, as well as their families.

B. What Are the Tax Disadvantages?

Professional corporations may involve some tax disadvantages, compared to operation in the form of a partnership or sole proprietorship.

1. Social Security Taxes

By making the professional himself an employee of the corporation, the tax treatment with respect to FICA Withholding (Social Security) Tax is different from that involved in the case of a self-employed person. In the case of a corporate employer, the employer and employee each pays one-half of the tax involved, and the total tax, in the case of a corporate employer, will exceed the Social Security Tax paid by the self-employed. On the maximum income subject to Social Security, $7,800, the tax will be $748.80 on the corporation and the employee together; whereas, the comparable tax for a self-employed person is only $538.20. The half of the tax paid by the corporation, $374.40, is, however, deductible.

2. State and Federal Unemployment Tax

The tax treatment of the professional as an employee will, in the case of a professional corporation, also cause somewhat greater taxes overall than in the case of a partnership or sole proprietorship, with respect to the state and federal unemployment tax. This tax, however, is so small that it is of no great significance.

3. Workmen's Compensation Rates

The same can be said of the increased workmen's compensation rates which will be applicable to the professional as a corporate employee. They will result in a slightly higher payment by the corporation to cover the professional under the workmen's compensation schedule.

4. Corporate Income May Be Taxed Twice

What would appear, at first blush, to be a considerable tax disadvantage of the professional corporation is the double taxation of corporate income, since it is taxed to the shareholder. Since professional corporations generally will not have sufficient income to cause dividends to be declared, this tax disadvantage, which can be very real in the case of ordinary corporations, is illusory at best in the case of professional corporations.

5. State and Local Income Taxes

The application of state and local income taxes to professional corporations is not likely to be of any great consequence, since the corporation will pay out virtually all of its income in the form of salary, bonuses and contributions to the pension and profit-sharing plans, as well as for the fringe benefits purchased for the benefit of the employees.

A professional corporation will, as a corporation under state law, be subject to state franchise taxes, and this may constitute a disadvantage, although state franchise taxes applicable to professional corporations are not likely to be of great moment compared to the substantial advantages involved with respect to Federal taxes.

There are some tax problems related to the Federal income tax treatment of corporations which deserve mention. They will be discussed in greater detail in Chapter 7.

6. Surtax on Unreasonable Accumulations of Earnings and Profits

If corporate profits are accumulated in excess of $100,000, there may possibly be a problem with the surtax on unreasonable accumulations of earnings and profits. The answer to this problem is a simple one—the corporation should not accumulate earnings and profits to this extent.

7. Personal Holding Company Tax Problem

There would be a personal holding company tax problem in the event that contracts entered into by the professional corporation permitted the patient or client of the professional corporation to stipulate the identity of the employee who is to perform the services involved. This problem can be solved by making sure that contracts to render services give the corporation the power to designate who will perform the services.

8. Is Compensation Paid to Corporate Employees Unreasonable and Therefore Not Deductible?

The question of whether compensation paid to corporate employees is unreasonable, and therefore not deductible, is not likely to be too serious for a professional corporation unless, under the facts, the compensation is not, in fact, earned by the employee to whom it is paid, or is commingled with income from other sources.

All in all, the tax disadvantages which can be conjured up in the case of a professional corporation are certainly small, at best, and hardly to be compared with the tax advantages of a professional corporation.

C.   What Are the Non-Tax Advantages?

The non-tax advantages of professional corporations are, while perhaps not as important as the tax advantages, nevertheless real and substantial.

The professional corporation brings with it six basic corporate attributes, which serve to distinguish corporations from partnerships, and each of them may, in a given instance, be of real value to the organization.

1. Management Is Centralized

A corporation, as distinguished from a partnership, has a greater degree of centralization of management. This is effected through the centralization of management in the Board of Directors, officers and Executive Committee. In the case of a professional corporation, it permits the shareholders to delegate management responsibilities and thereby devote greater time to their professional practice.

Why Incorporate the Professional Practice?

2. Liability Is Limited

The professional corporation may also result in a degree of limited liability which is not possible in the case of a partnership.

In the case of a partnership, every partner may enter into a contract which will bind his fellow partners as well as the firm. In the case of a professional corporation, however, where an officer of the corporation properly acts within the bounds of the authority given him by the Board of Directors, only the corporation will be liable. The liability of partners for torts committed by their fellow partners does not apply between shareholders of a professional corporation. Where one of the shareholders of a professional corporation gets into legal trouble, this will not involve his fellow shareholders, except to the extent of their interest in the corporate assets. In other words, the protection of the corporate shield is available to the professional owners as shareholders in a corporation.

3. There Is Greater Continuity of Organization

A professional corporation has the continuity of life which pertains to any corporation, as distinguished from a partnership.

In the case of a partnership, the firm, as a matter of law, comes to an end upon the death or incapacity of any partner. A professional corporation, on the other hand, being a corporation under state law, continues its existence regardless of the death, resignation, withdrawal, retirement, expulsion, incompetency or bankruptcy of any shareholder; moreover, no shareholder may, by himself, dissolve the corporation.

In the case of a professional corporation set up by a sole practitioner, the continuity of life of the corporation may be a very substantial factor, particularly in the case of a lawyer. On the death of the sole shareholder, the files of the client will belong to the corporation and will not pass through probate of the lawyer's estate. The same is true in the case of the patient file and records of a solo doctor. The client or patient, as the case may be, will know that, through the corporation, continuity will be provided, and his records will not belong to the estate of the deceased lawyer or doctor, but rather to the corporation. Of course in the case of a medical clinic or law firm where there are two or more shareholders, the continuity provided by the corporation will be much greater than in the case of the solo practitioner who incorporates.

4. Transferability of Interests Is Facilitated

A professional corporation has greater flexibility with respect to transfer of interests than does a partnership.

The transfer of corporate stock is a relatively simple matter; whereas, the transfer of a partnership interest is much more complicated. The corporation permits the setting up of a stock purchase and redemption agreement, which will provide a market to the older professional when the time comes to transfer his interest in the practice to younger members. This can provide a greater degree of safety to the older practitioner, and to his widow and family. For the younger practitioner, it provides greater assurance of his right to take over the practice and simplicity in accomplishing this objective.

A professional corporation may provide a much better medium for transfer of the professional practice from the older to the younger members (with favorable tax treatment), provision of the funds with which to do it and establishment of a definite value for the shares.

5. Employee Relations Are Improved

By virtue of the pension, profit-sharing and fringe benefits available to all of the employees of the professional corporation, there can be very substantial improvement in employee relations and loyalty to the enterprise. This will be further discussed in Chapter 5.

6. May Help as a Selling Point in Getting New Professionals to Join

These benefits may very well enable the professional corporation to compete in the market for young professionals to a degree not possible in the case of a partnership.

D. What Are the Non-Tax Disadvantages?

There may be some disadvantages to a professional corporation which are not related to taxes, but which in a given case may be considered important by the particular professionals involved.

Why Incorporate the Professional Practice?

1. Freedom Over Investments Is Less

While the professional corporation permits opportunity for investments with substantial tax advantages, it cannot be denied that the freedom of each professional over the investments may be more limited than is the case with investments made by him with respect to his funds left over after he has paid income tax on them. The individual professional may have entered into individual investments in real estate, stocks, and other securities, or ventures of various kinds, which he considers worthwhile and on which he may, in time, realize long-term capital gains. The contributions made by the corporation to the various investment programs of the professional corporation will take some of the money which he might otherwise use in those investments.

2. Some Professional People Don't Want to Retire

Another problem may arise with respect to retirement of the professional. It is possible that he may not live to retire, in which event it would appear that some of the pension benefits might be lost, and certainly lost to him personally. On the other hand, some professional people feel that they do not ever want to retire and, consequently, retirement benefits may, to them, seem of no great value. In answer to these points, it might be noted that even though the professional does not live to enjoy his retirement, he can, if the plan so provides, designate the benefits to go to his wife or other beneficiaries. The professional who does not plan to retire may, in time, find that whether he wishes or not, he must retire, due to accident, illness, loss of professional skill, senility, incompetency, loss of confidence in him on the part of others or because of other circumstances beyond his control. In such event, the lack of retirement benefits to ease his forced retirement can prove to be most unfortunate.

3. It Requires a Change in Professional Habits and Outlook

Another problem arises in connection with the habits and outlook of some professional people. We are all creatures of habit and some professional people simply do not want to change their partnership or sole proprietorship form of doing business, regardless of the benefits that might come from incorporation. In addition, in the case of some professional organizations, such as large law firms, there may be special problems in-

39

volved with older partners who have a large interest in partnership profits and do not wish to change their status to that of employees.

4. The Special Problems for Large Law Firms

Some professionals want to spend all they earn. In their case, no amount of tax and other advantages will persuade them to change their scale of living. They want to "live it up" and "the devil take the hindmost." In the case of some professionals, particularly in the first years of their practice, their education has been so tiring and difficult that they are simply tired of being poor. Now that they are making some money, they, and their wives also, may want to live as well as their means permit, and perhaps even better. Their education, the arrival of children and then their purchase of a home, cars, and other items that they want, whether it be a necessity or a luxury, may have resulted in debt that permits no leeway for contributions to retirement plans, in any amount whatsoever. Virtually every large group that considers incorporation has at least one member who has difficulty seeing how, attractive as the retirement and other benefits may be, he can spare the dollars from his paycheck to provide those benefits for himself, let alone for the other employees of the organization. Professional corporations simply are not for all professionals—only those who feel they can afford them. It goes without saying that the professional who is having a hard time of it financially, or for that matter who simply is not making a substantial income, may well, with good reason, decide to defer action. No real cut-off point can be set, since each case must be resolved on its own facts.

5. Is There an Ethics Question?

While the question of whether professional people may ethically operate in corporate form has been given a great deal of attention, there would seem to be no problem at this time. As a practical matter, the professional practice must, by state law, be confined to the individual professional. His relationship to his client or patient must remain inviolate and confidential, although the organization in which he functions may take the form of a corporation under state law.

6. Disclosure Requirements

Corporations are sometimes subject to greater governmental regulation and may be required to provide greater information to governmental agencies and to the general public than would be true of partnerships and proprietorships. To this extent, operating in corporate form would appear to have a possible disadvantage in terms of disclosure requirements.

Whether the non-tax disadvantages are sufficient to outweigh the tax and non-tax advantages resulting from professional incorporations must, of course, be decided on the particular facts. It may well be, that in a given case, a particular non-tax disadvantage may substantially, if not completely, in the judgment of the professional involved, offset all of the advantages which might be obtained by incorporation. In most cases, certainly, it would not appear to be this way, but each case must be resolved in the light of the particular people and circumstances involved.

E. Why Not Adopt a Keogh Plan Instead?

Keogh or H.R. 10 Plans have the virtue of simplicity. They do not, however, begin to compare in their benefits, in most cases, with the professional corporation.

1. Contributions Are Limited

In the case of a Keogh Plan, the contributions are limited to 10% of the earned income or $2,500 per year, whichever is less. In the case of a corporate plan, contributions may, if the corporate income warrants, be made considerably in excess of these amounts. In the case of corporate plans, contributions to profit-sharing plans may be made up to 15% of the compensation of the eligible employees. In the case of pension plans, there is no fixed limit, other than what the plan provides, if it is properly constituted, and actuarially sound. Where both a pension and a profit-sharing plan are involved, the contribution is limited to 25% of the compensation of the eligible employees in the first year, although an additional 5% may be contributed and deducted as a carryover in the following year.

In the case of Keogh Plans, an owner-employee may make voluntary contributions to the plan if he has at least one common-law employee who is covered by the plan, but the voluntary contribution by the owner-employee on his own behalf is limited to 10% of his own compensation or $2,500, whichever is less. In the case of a corporate plan, voluntary contributions are limited to 10% of compensation. Accordingly, a professional who has a corporate plan may make voluntary contributions to the plan, in addition to those made by the corporation, up to 10% of his compensation, and the amounts contributed by him will build up free of tax under the corporate plan, together with the contributions of the corporation.

Keogh Plans, by distinguishing between those owners of the business who own more than 10%, as compared with those who own less than 10%—that is, the "owner-employees" and the "self-employed," respectively—bring about discriminatory treatment as between partners. For example, if two partners each earn $40,000 per year, but one of them owns 10% or more in the firm and the other owns less than 10%, then the firm may contribute $4,000 for one of the partners, but only $2,500 for the other. In the case of each partner, however, only a $2,500 tax deduction may be taken. The "self-employed" individuals, who are not "owner-employees," in that they are not sole proprietors, or do not own more than 10% capital or profits interest in a partnership of which they are members, are not subject to the $2,500 limitation which applies to contributions. Thus, if they have sufficient earned income to permit a contribution in excess of $2,500, it may be made. However, while this is true of contributions, it is not true of the amounts which they may deduct for income tax purposes, and in this respect such self-employed individuals are subject to the same limitations as owner-employees. There is, nevertheless, an advantage in being able to contribute amounts in excess of $2,500, in that the increment on such amounts will not be taxable until actual distribution is made at the end of the accumulation period.

Penalties are provided under Keogh Plans for excessive contributions. If the "self-employed" person receives notification from the Internal Revenue Service that his contribution was excessive, he must retrieve the excess within six months, together with the income earned on it. For this purpose, an excess contribution is an amount which exceeds the total of: (1) allowable contributions, upon which the deductible amount is based, and (2) permitted voluntary contributions, which in no case are deductible.

Why Incorporate the Professional Practice?

2. Integration with Social Security Is Restricted

Another problem with the Keogh Plans lies in the fact that they may not be integrated with Social Security if more than one-third of the deductible contributions are for the owner-employees; whereas, corporate plans may be integrated with Social Security. The net effect is that non-discriminatory contributions may be made to pension plans with respect to compensation not subject to Social Security. If there are both a pension and a profit-sharing plan, only one plan may be integrated. The differential in treatment between compensation subject to Social Security and that which is not, may not, in profit-sharing plans, exceed 6%.

3. Contributions Must Vest Immediately

In a Keogh Plan, contributions must vest immediately when made. In a corporate plan, contributions can be vested according to a selected schedule and over a period of years.

In the case of corporate retirement plans, it is general practice to provide that an employee must remain employed for a specified period of years before his interest in the plan becomes nonforfeitable. Generally, a profit-sharing plan provides a graduated scale over a period of years, during which time a specified portion of such employee's interest vests and becomes nonforfeitable. While there is a minimum vesting period provided under a corporate retirement plan, the forfeitures resulting may provide a considerable advantage to those employees who stay with the employer. They may not, however, be allocated on a basis which discriminates in favor of the officers or higher-paid, shareholder or supervisory employees.

The vesting provisions of Keogh Plans run counter to one of the principal reasons for retirement plans; namely, to encourage employees to stay with the employer. Once an employee under the Keogh Plan has accumulated some interest under the plan, the existence of this interest, providing a ready source of money to the employee if he leaves the employer, can become an inducement to leave rather than to stay. In the case of a corporation, the vesting provisions with respect to profit-sharing plans can sometimes work this way as well, and there have even been instances where corporate employees have used their vested interest under a profit-sharing plan to provide them with the starting capital to enter a new business in competition with their old employer.

43

4. The Trustee Must Be a Bank

In a Keogh Plan, the trustee must be a bank or trust company, unless the funds are invested in an annuity, endowment or life insurance contract or government bonds. In corporate plans, there is great flexibility with respect to the selection of the trustee. Even though the fund, under Keogh Plans, has a corporate trustee, transactions by the trustee with owner-employees who hold more than a 10% interest are severely restricted, and loans from the fund to such owner-employees, as well as any property transactions between them and the trust fund, are prohibited.

5. All Regular Employees with Three Years' Service Must Be Included

In Keogh Plans, all regular employees with three or more years of service must be included in the plan. Under corporate plans, if at least 70% of the employees are eligible and at least 80% of those eligible are included, then the plan will be qualified. The plan may be limited to certain categories of employees, if it does not discriminate in favor of shareholders, officers and highly compensated or supervisory employees. Under corporate retirement plans, it is possible to require up to five years' service to be eligible for the plan, as well as to set minimum ages for qualification. In addition, plans may exclude certain classes of employees, such as hourly paid workers or those covered by a union-negotiated plan, but not if this constitutes discrimination against them.

6. Distributions Are Taxed as Ordinary Income, Subject to Averaging

Under Keogh Plans, the distributions are all subject to tax as ordinary income, and are subject to an averaging formula computed on a five-year basis. Distributions in one taxable year, under a corporate plan, will be subject to capital gains tax, to the extent of the income and growth of the trust fund, while contributions of the employer will be taxed to the employee as ordinary income, subject to averaging on a seven-year basis. It has become somewhat of a bromide to sum up Keogh Plans as the best way yet to convert capital gains into ordinary income. Under a Keogh Plan an "owner-employee"—that is, one who has more than a 10% interest —may not be paid any benefit prior to the time he reaches the age of 59½ years, except in case of death or total disability. Benefit payments must, in any event, begin before he reaches the age of 70½. In the case of all other persons covered under a Keogh Plan, the distribution of such employee's interest must be made or begun not later than the year he reaches 70½ years or the year in which he retires, whichever is later.

In the case of ordinary corporate retirement plans, broad discretion is usually given to the trustee to determine the method of distribution which will be best adapted to the needs of the individual employee, after he terminates his employment. Provisions are generally made for early, normal or late retirement.

Under a Keogh Plan, on the other hand, there can be no provision for distributions to 10% interest holders in case of emergency, nor can there be any provision for early retirement or for distribution on termination of the plan before he reaches the age of 59½ years. Premature distributions are subject to penalty. In the case of premature distribution, no further contributions may be made for the self-employed for five years thereafter, and, in addition, a tax penalty equal to 10% of the increase in tax resulting from the distribution is imposed on the self-employed person receiving the distribution.

7. Benefits Are Subject to Estate Tax

Another substantial disadvantage of Keogh Plans for professional people lies in the fact that the benefits under the plan are not exempt from Federal estate tax; whereas, the benefits under corporate plans are not subject to Federal estate tax.

Under Keogh, the self-employed cannot qualify for the $5,000 death benefit, which, in the case of corporate retirement plans, may be made, free of estate tax, to the widow, estate or designated beneficiaries of an employee.

If any confirmation of the disenchantment of professionals with Keogh Plans was needed, it is certainly provided by the Treasury statistics for 1970 when compared with 1969. In 1969 a total of approximately 100,-000 Keogh Plans were approved by the Service. In 1970, the total was only 401, or less than .5% of the total for 1969. In other words, the adoption of Keogh Plans virtually came to a complete halt in 1970. In contrast, the number of employee benefit plans for corporate employees increased from approximately 28,000 in 1969 to 32,500 in 1970. Is it any wonder, then, that those professionals who give the matter any substantial thought will choose the corporate plan rather than the Keogh Plan when they have a free choice.

F. Effect of 1969 Tax Reform Act

Some changes in the tax law which can affect the decision as to whether or not to incorporate a professional practice are contained in the provisions of the Tax Reform Act of 1969.

1. 50% Ceiling on Earned Income

One of these changes is found in the 50% ceiling on the tax rate applicable to earned income. Effective in 1972, earned income will be subject to a top rate of 50%. There is a limitation on this, however, since it does not apply to other types of income. If a professional has substantial amounts of income from investments or another business, the income from those sources will be subject to the higher bracket. Moreover, the earned income, which would be limited to the 50% bracket (60% in 1971), would be removed from the benefit of the ceiling to the extent that the professional has "tax preference" income of various kinds.

2. Special 10% Tax on "Tax Preference" Income

The 1969 Tax Reform Act introduced a special 10% tax on "tax preference" income. Included in such income are excess investment interest, the untaxed portion of capital gains, accelerated depreciation, the excess of percentage depletion over otherwise allowable depletion and stock options. To the extent that the tax preference items exceed $30,000, plus the taxpayer's income tax liability for the year, the tax preference income is made subject to the special 10% tax. The professional who might be eligible for the 50% limitation on earned income with respect to his compensation—the tax preference income, if over $30,000 in the taxable year, as well as in excess of that amount, on average, for the four preceding taxable years—will lose, to that extent, the benefit of the maximum limitations of tax on his earned income for the year.

3. Increased Tax Rate on Long-Term Capital Gains

Another factor to be taken into account, as a result of the Tax Reform Act of 1969, is the increase in tax rate on long-term capital gains in excess of $50,000 in any one year. For 1971, the rate on capital gains, in such case, will be 32.5% and 35% for 1972 and thereafter. For a professional taxpayer who has invested in capital gain items, such as securities and real estate, for example, over a period of years, looking forward to disposing of those assets at favorable capital gain rates, the new and higher rates on capital gains over $50,000 can prove quite frustrating. If those same properties were owned by a pension or profit-sharing trust, there would be no capital gain tax on the sale.

4. Limitation on Subchapter S Corporations

A further tax problem created by the Tax Reform Act of 1969 is found in the limitation on Subchapter S corporations, requiring that a shareholder-employee include in his taxable income contributions made to a qualified plan on his behalf, to the extent that they exceed $2,500 or 10% of his compensation, whichever is less.

G. Future Treasury Legislative Plans

In trying to decide whether to incorporate or not, the professional people are still faced with the problem of deciding what the Treasury Department plans to do. For years this has posed a problem in the form of Treasury Regulations directed against professional corporations and associations. After the passage of the Tax Reform Act of 1969, the problem has not been one of trying to predict the form of the Treasury Regulations but rather to predict what plans the Treasury Department might present to Congress for wholesale changes in pension and profit-sharing plans for corporations generally.

1. Limitation on Contributions by Owner-Employee Taxpayers

There have been indications that the Treasury Department would, at some future time, propose to Congress that all owner-employee taxpayers, as defined in H.R. 10—that is, shareholders owning more than a 10% interest in the corporation—should be limited in their contributions to retirement plans to one-sixth of their annual income, with a top limit of $10,000 per year, or four times the amount provided in the Keogh Plan.

2. Restriction of Retirement Benefits

A further limitation would restrict retirement benefits to 3% of an employee's final pay, multiplied by his years of service, or 4% in the case of career salary plans, but with his pay restricted to a top limit of $60,000 for this purpose. In addition, a limited amount, perhaps $1,000, would be permitted for an employee's own voluntary contributions to his pension plan, but this would not, perhaps, apply to voluntary contributions by owner-employees.

3. Keogh Plan Limitations on Vesting, Coverage, Contributions and Distributions Applied to Corporate Plans Generally

Many of the Keogh Plan limitations on vesting, coverage, contributions and distributions would be applied to corporate plans generally. The proposed vesting provisions, which would be made applicable to all qualified plans, would impose a "rule of 50," which would provide that an employee whose age and service equal 50—as for example, an employee age 35, with 15 years of service—would vest at such point 50%, and an additional 10% each year thereafter. Where the ratio of non-owner-employees to owner-employees is less than 2 to 1, then a "rule of 35" would be imposed, so that 50% vesting would occur when any combination of age and service adds up to 35. Many of the field offices of the Internal Revenue Service have been imposing special vesting rules on pension and profit-sharing plans of professional corporations which require earlier vesting than do ordinary corporate plans. This has been imposed as the price by each field office for a determination letter with respect to the particular plan.

4. Elimination of Estate Tax Exclusion for Qualified Plans Under Section 2039(c) of the Code

A further modification of the present rules with respect to qualified pension and profit-sharing plans of corporations appears in the Treasury proposal that the estate tax exclusion for qualified plans under Section 2039(c) of the Code be eliminated. Whether such a proposal, if adopted by Congress, would apply to existing plans remains to be seen. Certainly the estate tax exemption has been a factor in encouraging employers to adopt qualified plans in the past, but the Treasury apparently feels that the estate tax preferential treatment of qualified plans, as compared with other types of property owned by a decedent at the time of his death, can no longer be justified. Whether Congress will agree with that will remain to be seen. In this proposal, the Treasury is seeking to apply to corporate plans the same treatment accorded Keogh Plans under the law at the present time.

The uncertain nature of the Treasury's proposals, coupled with the additional uncertainty as to whether Congress would enact the Treasury proposals when proposed, certainly makes the Treasury plans for the future a factor "X" in the picture. The Treasury proposals are further discussed in Chapter 8. Whether a particular professional should wait "until the smoke has settled" is, of course, an individual decision.

H. "To Be or Not to Be"—We Know the Question, But What Is the Answer?

In seeking to answer the question of whether a professional should incorporate, all of the factors previously discussed will need to be considered, both tax and non-tax. Whether the tax advantages discussed previously will prevail in a particular situation will depend, to a large extent, on the tax bracket in which the professional finds himself.

1. How Do You Weigh the Factors?

The higher his bracket, the more he is likely to be influenced toward incorporation. The income he has from other investments will also enter the picture. Offsetting the tax advantages of incorporation are some very slight tax disadvantages, although they should all be considered. In addition, the non-tax advantages and disadvantages will each need to be weighed in the light of all the facts in the particular situation. The nature of the individuals involved must be carefully considered. Some professionals, for whom incorporation would involve considerable tax advantage, nevertheless are unable to restrict themselves to the disciplines that are involved in putting aside from earned income amounts for retirement, saving and insurance benefits which come with incorporation. In some cases, incorporation may come too late in the practicing lifetime of the professional. In the case of a group, it may well be that one or two professionals may choose to stay out of the pension or profit-sharing plan. This can be done; whereas, to leave out non-shareholders, could result in discrimination which would disqualify the pension or profit-sharing plan.

2. Is There a Ready Answer?

It becomes clear that there is no one pat answer to the question of whether one should or should not incorporate. It becomes necessary in each case to weigh all of the factors, pro and con, and then the judgment decision must be made by those who would become the shareholders of the corporation. In making this decision they must bear in mind that the decision, once made, cannot be lightly set aside, since undertaking the pension or profit-sharing plan involves continuing obligations upon the corporation. In making the decision, the shareholder-employees will need constant professional help to delineate and evaluate the benefits and the risks, as well as the cost involved. A more comprehensive discussion of this question is undertaken in Chapter 9.

3. What Has Been the Experience of Doctors with Incorporation?

Until the publication of the results of a survey of the medical profession,[1] there were no worthwhile statistics on what has been happening with incorporation in any profession. Since the medical profession has been more active in this respect than any other, the figures for that profession are, not surprisingly, the first to be made available. They indicate that of the some 14,000 doctors surveyed, approximately one doctor in 12 is now operating in corporate form, either by himself or as part of an incorporated group. It also appears that the doctors, on the average, are putting into profit-sharing and pension plans approximately one-sixth of their income. Indications are that the doctors have found that, by incorporating, they are forced to budget their finances, not only for taxes, but for other purposes as well. An interesting fact brought out in the survey is that one

---

[1] William A. Levinson, "What Incorporation Has Done for Doctors," *Medical Economics,* May 24, 1971, p. 83.

out of nine incorporated doctors is earning less than $30,000 per year, so it appears that incorporation is not confined to the extremely prosperous doctors, although the survey does indicate that the higher the doctor's income, the more he is likely to put into the pension or profit-sharing plan. While "one swallow does not a summer make," nevertheless it appears that doctors are incorporating in ever increasing numbers, and those who have incorporated appear to be very happy with their decision to do so.

4. Should Your Conscience Hurt You?

One of the main stumbling blocks in the way of professionals who have considered incorporation has been the problem of conscience. Many have insisted on donning the hair shirt. This matter has been largely twofold in nature. One aspect of it relates to professional ethics, the other to governmental attitude.

(a) *Does a Professional Corporation Violate Rules of Ethics?*

A tremendous amount of ink has been spread on the question of whether incorporation of a professional practice constitutes a violation of professional ethics. All of the professional corporation and association statutes have been drafted with careful delineation between the conduct of the professional practice as such and the organization of the business end of the practice. There is really no conflict, and the answer is clear. Professional practice, whether it be medical, legal, accounting or some other profession, is confined to those who are licensed to practice the profession. The form of organization, whether it be sole proprietorship, partnership, corporation or association, has nothing to do with the conduct of the professional practice, per se. The practice is limited to human beings who must be licensed by the proper authorities of the state for the particular profession involved. No one else may practice the profession, nor may anyone else control the licensed professional in the conduct of his practice. The organization of the business end of the practice has absolutely nothing to do with the control of the practice of the profession itself.

(b) *Is There Something Immoral About Professional Corporations?*

Another facet of the over-active conscience on the professional incorporation question has been evidenced by members of Congress and some of the spokesmen for the Treasury Department over the past few years.

Why Incorporate the Professional Practice?

The implication is that some professionals are highly overpaid, and anything that gives them a semblance of tax equality may be open to criticism as a "loophole" or special privilege for highly paid professionals. This was the basis for the attack by some members of the Senate Finance Committee, during the course of the consideration of the Tax Reform Bill in 1969, when the Committee voted to restrict contributions to professional corporations to the limitations ($2,500 per year or 10% of income), as in the case of Keogh Plans. Some of the same thinking appears to under-ride the Treasury Department's proposals for a fixed limit on contributions to pension and profit-sharing plans, discussed in Part G of this chapter. Should the professional's conscience hurt him if he is highly successful in his professional practice and if the proposed professional corporation might achieve very substantial tax benefits for him?

(c) *How Does the Professional Corporation Compare with Congressional Benefits?*

Perhaps the conscience-stricken professional might feel a little better when he considers the benefits which the members of Congress have conferred on themselves.[2] Members of Congress, in addition to their base salary of $42,500 per year, are entitled to pension benefits of as much as $34,000 a year for life. In addition, they have a host of other fringe benefits which make the benefits from professional incorporation pale into insignificance. Among these fringe benefits can be found $42,500 in life insurance, at special rates, plus a widow's benefit equal to one year's salary or $42,500. In addition, medical care and special hospitalization rates are provided; travel allowances, including free trips to foreign countries; the use of government transportation; rental allowances and a government-subsidized health-insurance plan. When compared to the treatment the members of Congress accord themselves, the tax benefits to be derived by a professional from his incorporation are small indeed. Without in any way attacking the wisdom or the rectitude of Congress in providing these privileges for its own members, it does seem clear that a professional who is considering incorporation should certainly not let himself be burdened with a hair-shirt conscience, based on thoughts that he might thereby be doing too much for himself or his family. If the congressional yardstick is

---

[2] *U.S. News and World Report*, March 22, 1971.

52

any measure, then the answer to the question of whether the professional should be bothered by a guilty conscience when he forms a professional corporation would seem to have a clear and emphatic answer in the negative.

(d) *Is Social Security the "Better Way"?*

If any further argument were needed, it can be supplied by a quick look at what has been happening to Social Security. The base is rapidly approaching $10,200 and the Social Security tax is already being elevated above the 14% minimum income tax bracket, with no indication that the increase in Social Security tax and benefits has any foreseeable limit. It appears that to many of those wishing to impose severe limitations on professional corporations government-supplied and government-controlled Social Security is commendable, but for the citizens to provide for their own security through the private pension and profit-sharing system is to be frowned upon. Unfortunately, the source from which both the government-controlled Social Security plan and the private pension and profit-sharing plan must obtain their funds is the same; namely, the profits of the particular private enterprise. To the extent that those funds go to the government-controlled plan, they are not available to the private plan. It appears that to some this means that the private plan must give way, since the government plan, for some unexplained reason, is to them better and has a built-in moral advantage of some sort.

2

How Do You Go About
Organizing the Corporation?

A. Should It Be a Corporation or an Association?

Assuming that a group of professional people who have been operating as a partnership wish to obtain corporate benefits, the obvious question is, how do they go about organizing? And what is it they organize? The answer to this will lie in the provisions of the particular state law.

1. What Do the State Laws Provide?

The laws of nine states provide for professional associations by specific statutory provisions; whereas, the laws of the other states provide for professional corporations. It will be necessary in each instance to see what the laws of the particular state provide. The nine states providing for professional associations are Alabama, Georgia, Illinois, Nevada, New Hampshire, Ohio, South Carolina, Texas and Virginia. In all the other states, the laws provide for professional corporations. In some of the states where the entities are called "associations" they are actually corporations. Texas provides for associations for the medical profession and corporations for all other professions. In some states, the laws are limited to particular professions, and in a number of states there are separate laws for different professions. For example, in Minnesota there are five such statutes, each for a separate profession, and all virtually identical. Accordingly, one must first look at the law which is provided in the particular state and see whether the statute provides for professional associations or professional corporations. Then one will need to determine whether the particular profession in question is covered by the statute. Even if it is not, there is a possibility that a common law association may be established, even though there may be no specific statute providing for an association or corporation for that particular profession.

2. What Difference Does It Make Whether It Is a Corporation or an Association?

One might well ask at this point, what is the difference between an association and a corporation, and what significance will there be as to whether the particular state law provides for associations or for corporations?

Without going into considerable detail and history at this point, it may suffice to note that in the *Empey* case,[1] involving a law firm in Colorado, as well as in *United States v. O'Neill*,[2] involving an association of Ohio doctors, the Circuit Courts of Appeal held that an entity which is a corporation under state law is also a corporation for Federal tax purposes. In a later case, *Kurzner v. United States*,[3] decided by the Fifth Circuit later in the same year, the Court held that a corporation formed by two Florida doctors, under the Professional Service Corporation Act of that state, was taxable as a corporation under the Federal tax law, but not because it was a corporation under state law. The Court in that case based its decision on the ground that the corporation had the four basic corporate attributes which the Supreme Court of the United States had stated in the *Morrissey*[4] case, in 1935, would serve to make an association taxable as a corporation. Those characteristics are: (1) centralized management; (2) continuity of life; (3) limited liability; (4) transferability of interests.

On August 8, 1969, the Treasury Department, in TIR 1019, stated

---

[1] Empey v. United States (CCA 10, 1969).
[2] O'Neill v. United States (CCA 6, 1969).
[3] Kurzner v. United States (CCA 5, 1969).
[4] Morrissey v. Comm'r, 296 U.S. 344 (1935).

that it would no longer litigate the question of professional corporations and associations where they are properly organized under state law. In Rev. Rul. 70-101,[5] in March 1970, the Treasury Department specifically recognized the particular state statutes with respect to professional associations and corporations and stated that corporations and associations formed under those statutes would be treated as corporations for tax purposes. With the exception of special problems related to some old Pennsylvania and Illinois association laws and the Texas Professional Association Act, as to which specific rulings would be required, Rev. Rul. 70-101 stated that the Treasury Department would now recognize both professional corporations and associations which are formed in accordance with the applicable state law. The Service has recently ruled that a professional service association, organized and operated under the old Pennsylvania law, with centralized management, continuity of life and a modified form of free transferability, would be taxed as a corporation.[6]

One might ask, why are the state laws so varied? The answer to that is that they developed over a period of years and, in the beginning, the laws were all association statutes. Until the sixties it was felt by some that to permit the incorporation of a professional practice would interfere with the ethical relationship between the professional person and his patient or client. In one state, Pennsylvania, which had an antiquated partnership association law, the old law was repealed by the Professional Corporation Law in 1970.[7] In other states, such as Texas, while both a Professional Association Act for doctors of medicine and a Professional Corporation Act, for all the other professions, were adopted in 1969, the provisions of the old law enabling the formation of "common law" associations were still retained. Provision was made in the new Professional Association Act, however, for professionals organized as associations under the old laws to bring themselves into conformity with the new statutes.

One might also ask the further question, which form of organization is better, the association or the corporation? In a sense, that is answered for each state by the legislature in making its decision. From the standpoint of the solo practitioner, it would appear that the corporation

---

[5] Rev. Rul. 70-101, 1970 I.R.B. No. 9, p. 13.
[6] Rev. Rul. 71-277, 1971-26 I.R.B., 92.
[7] Act No. 160, Aug. 8, 1970.

law might be better, since there can be no question that you can have a one-man corporation; whereas, a one-man association might appear, to those who do not favor it, to pose philosophical, if not legal, problems. In the case of professionals who are engaged in a multi-state practice, it would appear that perhaps the association has the edge, since the professional corporation statutes generally restrict the activities of the corporation by requiring that the shareholders be duly licensed in the state of incorporation. An association, like a partnership, would have less problems crossing state lines than would a corporation, since a professional corporation organized in one state would have difficulty obtaining permission to do business in another state, unless it did that business through professionals who were licensed in the other state. This is a problem which will require careful consideration and, perhaps, in time, further implementation under the professional corporation statutes. It would seem likely that in time a uniform professional corporation statute, adopted by most, if not all, states, would be a logical development, as has been the case in the uniform state laws adopted in many other fields of the law.

In a number of states, and in certain professions, such as architecture, professional people have been able to incorporate under the business corporation act of the state. This is true, for example, with respect to architects in the state of Texas.

Another alternative which has been employed in a number of specific cases of medical clinics, is the formation of a charitable non-profit corporation which receives all the profits of the clinic after the doctors have received their compensation, in the form of salaries and bonus, and after payments to the retirement plan for the doctors and other employees of the clinic. A number of these situations had received Treasury Department approval at a time when the Treasury regulations still took the position that professional associations and corporations were, for Federal tax purposes, partnerships.

B. Who May Incorporate?

As we have already noted, all professional people who are specifically provided for in the particular state statute may set up either an association or a corporation, depending upon which is provided by the state law. If the particular profession is included by the state law, then the state statute will be adequate. If a particular profession is not provided for by the state law, then all that may be available to the particular profession would be to form a common law association and give the association the necessary corporate characteristics which were set forth by the Supreme Court in the *Morrissey* case. The question may then be asked, can this be done for the one-man association? How about the one-man association when we have a statute providing for it? May the one man bring in another member of his profession as a nominal associate? We do not have all the answers to these questions. They are discussed in Part I, 3 of Chapter 3.

1. What Is Included in "the Same Profession"?

The state laws providing for associations and corporations generally limit an association or a corporation to the members of "the same profession." In other words, doctors may not incorporate with lawyers; architects may not incorporate with accountants. To determine who are members of the "same" profession, one must ascertain the method of determining that question under the laws of the particular state. This may pose problems where a professional may be qualified in two professions; for example, a Certified Public Accountant, who is also a member of the bar, or an architect who is also an engineer. In Tennessee, Mississippi and Kansas, architects and engineers may join together. In Missouri, they are given a choice of doing so under either the general corporation law or the professional corporation act. In New York, engineering, architecture, landscape architecture or land surveying may be engaged in by the same professional corporation. Kansas also permits doctors of medicine and dentistry to join. Georgia permits engineers, architects and surveyors to join. Iowa goes to the extent of approving any combination that would be permitted with individuals or partnerships. Texas has recently removed from its Professional Association Act the limitation to one professional service.

An interesting provision is contained in the new Pennsylvania Professional Corporation Act which specifically provides that a professional corporation may be incorporated to render two or more kinds of professional services. To do so requires that the shareholders could have conducted a combined practice were they organized as a partnership, and provided that the appropriate regulating agency in each profession has expressly authorized the combined practice of such professions.

How Do You Go About Organizing the Corporation?

2. What Is the Role of the License?

Whether a person is a member of the same profession as the corporation or association involved can be determined by whether he has been duly licensed or admitted to practice his profession by the responsible agency which determines professional qualifications for that profession in the state. Generally, the statutes provide that the obtaining of a license is a condition precedent to the performance of the particular professional service.

Under the statutes, a professional person who loses his license to practice his profession will not only be disqualified professionally, but he will not be permitted to own stock or an interest in the professional corporation or association. The licensing procedure provides a means for policing the professional corporation or association and limits the benefits of the entity to those persons who are duly and properly licensed and thereby authorized to practice the profession.

3. What Happens if a Professional Is Disqualified?

Where a professional who was qualified to practice a particular profession dies, the statute will permit temporary ownership of the shares of the corporation or association by his estate, for a short period, generally not more than a year. Procedures for the purchase of the shares from his estate by the corporation are generally set forth in some detail in the statute. In the case of some statutes, the failure of the corporation to acquire from the estate of a deceased or disqualified shareholder the shares which he has held may result in forfeiture of the charter of the corporation. In some states, an alternative disposition to a person having the necessary qualifications in the profession is permitted. Many of the statutes expressly forbid any vesting of the voting rights in persons other than other shareholders or other members of the profession.

4. How Many Incorporators Are Required?

Generally, the corporation statutes of the state will require at least three incorporators. In the case of professional corporations, however, most of the statutes permit incorporation by one person who is a member of the profession. He becomes the sole officer and director of the corporation. While this may be a departure from the general rule with respect to ordinary corporations, nevertheless the law appears to be quite well settled that if the state law so provides, as long as the entity is a corporation under state law it will be considered to be a corporation for Federal income tax purposes.

C. What Special Problems Are Presented by the Professional Corporation?

The formation of a professional corporation or association may present a number of problems which, because of the fact that it is a profession that is involved, may require special consideration. They may not be covered by the general corporation statutes of the state.

1. How Does Incorporation Affect the Professional Relationship?

One might ask whether the formation of the corporation relieves the individual professionals of any of their responsibilities for their personal conduct in the practice of their profession. The Kentucky statute specifically provides that nothing in the statute shall restrict the board of competent jurisdiction to license persons to practice and to regulate the practice of the profession, even though the person involved is an officer, director, shareholder or employee of a professional corporation. May the corporation do things in its practice which would, if performed by an individual, constitute grounds for suspension of his right to practice? The statutes generally provide that the corporation may not do anything which would, if done by a licensed individual, violate the standards of professional conduct. They hold the individual professional responsible if he, by his act or omission, causes the corporation to violate the standards of professional conduct. Malpractice responsibility remains undiminished by the professional corporation. Disciplinary powers over licensed persons generally are specifically and expressly retained by the state statute authorizing professional corporations or associations. Since, however, the organization is a corporation or an association, the liability of the other members of the profession who are shareholders in the corporation or association will be limited to their interest in the corporation or association.

2. How Is Insurance to Cover Professional Liability Handled?

In some states, such as Colorado, the liability of the corporation and its shareholders for the acts, errors and omissions of the employees of the corporation will be protected by requiring that the corporation maintain professional liability insurance. In the Colorado Medical Corporation statute, a specific amount of insurance is provided for, as in the case of the Rule of Civil Procedure provision for law corporations. Whether a particular statute requires professional liability insurance or not, protection of the corporation and the individual professional practitioners involved certainly deserves careful attention so that adequate coverage may be enforced. It appears that in at least one state, California, the cost of such insurance for a professional corporation has been higher than in the case of a predecessor partnership, but there are indications that this extra cost may be reduced, or eliminated altogether.

3. How and When Does the General Business Corporation Act Apply?

In the case of some professions, as with architects in Texas, they may use the originary business corporation act. Generally the professional corporation statutes will provide that the general business corporation act will apply to the professional corporation, except to the extent that the provisions of the general business corporation act are inconsistent with the provisions of the professional corporation statute. Accordingly, all the burdens and benefits of corporations under state law will be imposed and conferred, including taxation under state law as a corporation. The professional corporation act will generally limit the activity of the professional corporation to the practice of the particular profession, except for the ownership of such property as may be appropriate or desirable in the rendering of the corporation's specific professional service.

4. What Will Be the Duration of the Corporation?

Since the professional corporation is in law a corporation, its life may be of such duration as is permitted for ordinary business corporations under state law. It may be organized for a specific period of years, or in perpetuity. Being a corporation, it is not limited to the life of a particular professional, or even all the professionals involved, although it must terminate when there is no professional shareholder alive to continue the corporation. In many states, annual registration is required.

How Do You Go About Organizing the Corporation?

5. How Is Dissolution of the Corporation Handled?

Dissolution of the professional corporation will be handled in the same fashion as applies to an ordinary business corporation under state law. Since there must be at least one duly licensed professional to own the shares of the corporation, if all of the shareholders die or are disqualified to practice their profession, then the corporation itself must terminate. The rights of creditors would be handled as in the case of an ordinary corporation under state law. In some states, as in California, for example, the professional corporation may become an ordinary corporation on the death of the last shareholder, by being required to cease rendering professional services.

6. Is the Stock Exempt from the Federal and State Securities Law?

In the absence of a special provision in the Professional Corporation Act, the corporation would appear to be subject to the provisions of the state blue sky law, as well as the Federal securities laws. It may well be that the normal exemptions provided in the securities acts of the state and the Federal law may eliminate any substantial problem in that regard.

7. Does the Term "Sole Purpose" Exclude Passive Investments?

The statute will generally state that the corporation is to be organized "for the purpose" of the particular profession. If other activities are to be engaged in, then the corporation will not be engaged in the purpose for which it was organized. Generally, as already noted, the professional corporation act will permit the professional corporation to own such real and personal property as may be necessary or appropriate for the fulfillment or rendering of the specific professional service or services which are involved. Quite often the act will specifically prohibit any other activity for the professional corporation. The ownership of passive investments which facilitate, or are necessary, or appropriate to, the practice of the profession, will not be a violation of the corporate purpose. The accumulation of substantial passive investments may, in time, however, bring about problems of unreasonable accumulation of earnings and profits under the Internal Revenue Code.

How Do You Go About Organizing the Corporation?

D. What Should the Articles of Incorporation Provide?

In organizing the corporation certain basic documents will be needed, the most important being, of course, the articles of incorporation, or charter, and the by-laws. In addition to those instruments, there will generally need to be some sort of agreement to permit the stock of the corporation to be bought and sold, employment agreements and sometimes medical expense reimbursement agreements.

1. The Purpose Clause

The purpose of the professional corporation will be restricted to the practice of the particular profession involved. While business corporations may have a broad spectrum of purposes, the professional corporation will be narrowly confined to the scope of the particular profession in which the shareholders are permitted to practice by virtue of their license granted by the state in their profession.

2. The Name of the Corporation

(a) *Use of Terms Such as "P.C." to Identify It as a Professional Corporation*

The statutes of the various states vary substantially with respect to the designation of the corporate name. In some cases they require the use of terms such as "P.C." or "P. A.," or other terms, such as "professional association," "professional corporation," "chartered," "incorporated" or "limited," denoting that it is a corporation or an association.

The Kentucky statute, for example, requires the use of the words "professional service corporation," "chartered" or the abbreviation "P.S.C."

(b) *Requirement That It Contain the Name of a Shareholder*

In some cases, the statute requires that the name contain the last name of a shareholder. This can present quite a serious problem for medical clinics, which may have operated for many years without using the name of any doctor in the firm name. They will have to comply with this provision or seek to have the statute changed by the legislature.

How Do You Go About Organizing the Corporation?

(c) *Use of Fictitious Name*

Where the name of a shareholder is not required by the statute, then it would seem that any name which serves to notify the public that it is in fact a corporation would be adequate. In some states, laws with respect to the practice of dentistry have specifically limited the use of names to the names of the individual or individuals licensed to practice dentistry. It would seem that the professional corporation act, having been enacted later in point of time, would modify the earlier statute. The safest course would, of course, be to follow the requirements of the particular professional corporation or association act of the state in all its specific details.

3. Who May Be Incorporators?

While ordinary corporations may be formed by incorporators who do not themselves become shareholders, in the case of professional corporations the incorporators must generally be members of the profession involved. Only licensed members of the profession may undertake to incorporate the professional practice. Generally, the statute will provide that they must be natural persons, duly licensed to practice the profession.

4. Who May Be Shareholders?

The role of shareholder in a professional corporation is limited to those who are duly licensed to practice the profession. Some statutes require that he be an employee, or formerly an employee. The corporation itself may, by acquiring shares from the licensed shareholders, become a shareholder. Upon the death of a shareholder, the shares generally must be purchased by the corporation and, if not, then by a duly licensed member of the profession. Similarly, if a shareholder becomes disqualified to practice the profession, his shares must be purchased from him.

5. Who May Be Directors?

The directors need not, in all states, be members of the profession. The Colorado medical statute, as an example, with respect to medical corporations, contemplates lay directors, but it expressly provides that they shall not exercise any authority whatsoever over professional matters. In most of the statutes, however, the directors must be members of the profession. In some, they must be a shareholder. In some statutes, provision is made to assure that there will be some rotation of the directors. This is accomplished by providing, in effect, that not all the shareholders may be directors at the same time. In Kentucky, where there is only one shareholder, he will be the sole incorporator and director and will fill all offices of the corporation.

6. Who May Be Officers?

Generally the officers may only be selected from shareholders. In the case of the Colorado statute, however, it is required that the president be a shareholder and a director and, "to the extent possible," all other directors and officers shall be persons who are licensed in the profession. Since a professional corporation is generally subject to the provisions of the business corporation law, except to the extent specifically excluded, provisions of the business corporation act, to the effect that the president and secretary may not be combined in the same person, will apply to professional corporations, as in the case of ordinary business corporations.

E.   What About the By-Laws?

1. Special Provisions for State Law Requirements

Each state professional corporation or association law has its own peculiarities. Many of these special requirements will need to be included in the by-laws. For example, the Kentucky statutory provisions as to purchase or redemption of shares might well be tracked in the by-laws. In the case of some statutes, as in the case of the Colorado law with respect to medical corporations, the by-laws could very well track the statute with respect to professional liability insurance. Provisions for filing with the Secretary of State, where required by the statute, could also be set forth in the by-laws. So could the procedures for the change from a predecessor partnership or association to a corporation, as, for example, in the Pennsylvania Corporation Act and the Texas Professional Association Act, each of which provides for adoption of the new act by existing professional partnership associations.

2. Basic Procedures for Corporate Operation

The by-laws, in the case of a professional corporation, constitute, as they do in the case of an ordinary business corporation, the basic procedures for operating the corporation. They will normally set forth the place of business of the corporation and provide for the corporate seal, the capital stock, the rights, powers and meetings of shareholders, the election of directors and officers and provision for their duties and their meetings. They will also provide for the method of handling corporate funds, books and records of the corporation and, in general, all of the normal requirements for conducting the corporate business.

F. What Can Be Done to Obtain an Ordinary Loss Deduction Through Use of a Section 1244 Provision?

1. What Is the Purpose of Such a Provision?

Since the Small Business Investment Act of 1958 was adopted, it has been possible for investors to obtain an ordinary loss deduction on investments in corporations which are small business corporations. The loss will be limited to $25,000 per year, or $50,000 on a joint return, where the holder of Section 1244 stock sells or exchanges it at a loss, or the stock becomes worthless. The benefits of the provision are only available to individuals and partnerships. While professional corporations, like other corporations, are only formed with a view toward making a profit, the inclusion of a Section 1244 provision at the outset may prove to be a great help taxwise in the event that the corporation proves to be a bad investment, since the loss, which would otherwise be only a capital loss, becomes an ordinary loss by virtue of the Section 1244 provision.

2. How Do You Make It a Small Business Corporation?

The procedure to be followed with respect to Section 1244 involves the adoption by the corporation of a plan which is in writing and adopted before the issuance of the shares. The plan should state the number of shares to be covered by the plan and the maximum amount to be paid for the stock. The stock must be common stock and the period of offering of the stock must not extend beyond two years from the date the plan was adopted. The stock must be issued only for money or other property, and the total of the capital and paid-in surplus may not exceed $500,000. The total stock which may be issued under the plan, plus the equity capital of the corporation at the time of adoption of the plan, may not exceed $1,000,000.

How Do You Go About Organizing the Corporation?

G. How Do You Handle the Stock Purchase Agreement?

In the case of professional corporations a stock purchase agreement, to enable a shareholder to sell his stock on the termination of his employment, or, in the event of his death, to permit his estate to sell his stock, is most essential. Such an agreement permits the shareholder or his estate to receive payment for his stock, according to the terms of the agreement, whether it be in a lump sum or over a period of years. Some of the professional corporation statutes set forth the redemption provisions in detail. They should be included in the articles of incorporation, the by-laws or in a separate agreement. The agreement will determine the value of the stock for estate tax purposes. The agreement is not only important as a part of the shareholder's estate planning, it also serves to prevent the ownership of stock of the corporation from staying in, or falling into, the hands of persons who are not licensed members of the profession.

1. Admission of New Stockholders

The stock purchase agreement provides a means for transferring ownership of stock from a withdrawing shareholder, or from the corporation, to a new shareholder. Such an agreement will generally provide a method of payment which will enable the new shareholder to acquire his stock over a period of time. The agreement may provide for the purchase of stock from the other shareholders, or from the corporation. In the latter event, provision will have to be made to comply with the state law which generally will provide that stock may only be issued for money, property or services which are actually rendered to the corporation. In the event that the new shareholder receives his stock for services, then he will have taxable compensation on which he must pay the income tax and the corporation will have a deduction.[8] If he receives the stock from another shareholder for services he will have taxable income, but the donor shareholder, unlike the corporation, will not be entitled to a deduction, because the new shareholder is not the donor shareholder's employee. If the stock is "restricted stock" under the Internal Revenue Code, as it generally will be in

---

[8] Rev. Rul. 62-217, 1962—2 C.B. 59.

a professional corporation, then, under the new rules set forth in the Tax Reform Act of 1969,[9] he will have ordinary taxable income on receipt of the stock for services, unless the stock is subject to "substantial risk of forfeiture." Even where the stock is subject to such risk, the employee receiving it may report it as income when received, provided he so elects within 30 days from the receipt by him of the stock.

2. Can You Fund It with Existing Life Insurance?

The use of life insurance to fund stock purchase agreements is a good solution to the problem presented when a shareholder dies and his stock has to be sold. The life insurance provides the corporation with the funds which it can use to pay the estate of the deceased shareholder for his stock. In determining the purchase price, this can be based upon some formula, such as the shareholder's pro rata portion of the assets of the corporation, less the liabilities, or it may be based upon a fixed value per share, or a determination by the accountants who handle the corporation's accounting, and in accordance with specified guidelines provided in the stock purchase agreement. Generally no value should be accorded to goodwill of the corporation, since this is best for the new stockholder. The selling stockholder can be compensated through retirement and other related benefits. The stock certificates should contain some endorsement indicating the existence of the agreement. Such an agreement may very well be subject to general state corporate law forbidding purchase by a corporation of its own stock except out of surplus.

3. How Is Voting Control Handled?

While shareholders will generally be permitted to set up a voting trust agreement which will enable certain shareholders to retain voting control, no such arrangement may be used to give the voting authority over the affairs of the corporation to someone who is not licensed to practice the particular profession involved. Some statutes contain a specific provision to this effect, but even in the absence of such a statutory provision a voting trust to give a non-qualified person authority over the affairs of the corporation would clearly be held invalid. An alternative method of

---

[9] Internal Revenue Code, Sec. 83.

handling the collective voting matter is for the shareholders to enter into a pooling agreement as to how they will vote on certain matters.

4. What Should the Stock Purchase Resolution Say?

Generally the stock purchase agreement will give the corporation or the shareholders priority rights to purchase the stock whenever a shareholder desires, or is required, to sell. Only when the corporation or the other shareholders have passed up this right will the selling shareholder, or his estate, be permitted to sell to someone else. Moreover, he or his estate may only sell to a purchaser who is licensed to practice the particular profession involved. The agreement will need to provide that it shall be binding not only upon the parties thereto, but also their successors and assigns.

H. Would Subchapter S Be of Any Value?

1. What Are the Requirements?

Subchapter S of the Internal Revenue Code provides that a corporation meeting the requirements of the Code will have its income taxed to the shareholders just as though they were partners. In order to take advantage of Subchapter S, however, certain requirements must be met.[10] Among those requirements are the following:

(1) The corporation must be a domestic corporation.
(2) The corporation may have no more than one class of stock outstanding.
(3) There must not be more than ~~ten~~ 25 shareholders.
(4) All of the shareholders must be individuals or estates. A trust cannot be a shareholder and the shareholders cannot be nonresident aliens.
(5) The shareholders must elect to be taxed as a small business corporation during the first month of the taxable year or the month preceding.

---

[10] Internal Revenue Code, Sec. 1371.

(6) Not more than 20% of the corporate income may be passive investment income; that is, income from royalties, rents, dividends, interest, annuities and sales or exchanges of stock or securities.

There are a few other requirements which are not, however, pertinent to a professional corporation, these relating to consolidated returns and income from sources outside the United States.

2. What Is the Effect of Subchapter S?

By electing to be a Subchapter S corporation, it is possible for the shareholders to have the income taxed to them as individuals, thus escaping corporate tax. Similarly, deductions can be passed through the corporation to the individual returns of the shareholders. As a result, many of the tax problems which relate to corporate income can be by-passed with a Subchapter S corporation. Among these problems are questions of unreasonable compensation, the personal holding company and unreasonable accumulation of earnings and profits. It, of course, also eliminates the double taxation of corporate income, since, in the case of a Subchapter S corporation, the income is taxed only to the shareholders themselves and not to the corporation. Accordingly, the shareholders will not have to receive the income in the form of dividends.

3. How Was It Affected by the Tax Reform Act of 1969?

The usefulness of Subchapter S for professional corporations was virtually vitiated by the requirement under the Tax Reform Act of 1969 that the shareholder-employee must include in his income the contributions made by a Subchapter S corporation where the contributions exceeded 10% of the compensation of the shareholder-employee or $2,500, whichever is less.[11] This, for practical purposes, imposed the same limitations as apply under H.R. 10 to Keogh Plans. A shareholder-employee is defined as an employee or officer who owns more than 5% of the corporation's stock. In addition, the Tax Reform Act of 1969 provided that a qualified stock-bonus or profit-sharing plan of a Subchapter S corporation

---

[11] Internal Revenue Code, Sec. 1379(b).

must provide that forfeitures allocable to deductible contributions may not inure to the benefit of shareholder-employees.[12]

The Tax Reform Act of 1969 did not make excessive contributions to a Subchapter S corporation plan subject to the same penalties as provided under H.R. 10. Such excessive contributions would not make the plan unqualified. Instead, the excess contributions must be included in the income of the shareholder-employee. The funds could, however, be left in the tax-exempt trust and thus would have the benefit of the tax-exempt growth, as a part of the profit-sharing or stock-bonus plan.

4. Is Subchapter S Worthwhile?

With the elimination of the opportunity to make contributions in excess of $2,500 per year to pension and profit-sharing plans brought about by the Tax Reform Act of 1969 restrictions, it would appear that the value of the Subchapter S corporation for a professional corporation would be virtually at an end.

Even without this severe limitation on contributions, it might be noted that Subchapter S corporations, while eliminating the double tax on dividends, and permitting the reflection of losses on the shareholders' individual tax returns, do involve the giving up of many tax benefits which could be afforded by the corporate form of doing business. Among these benefits, each of which needs to be considered in the light of all of the facts in a particular case, would be the splitting of income between the corporation and the shareholders, thereby taking advantage of the best possible balance in tax rates, as between the individual shareholders and the corporate rate. The Subchapter S election eliminates the opportunity to use the more favorable corporate 22% rate for the receipt of taxable income, as well as for the purchase of various types of insurance where the premiums are not deductible, as for example, in the case of split-dollar and key-man insurance.

The Subchapter S corporation definitely eliminates the opportunity to have different classes of stock in the same corporation, a matter of some importance where, for business purposes, it may be desirable to have fixed income going to certain shareholders on preferred stock, while giving other

---

[12] Internal Revenue Code, Sec. 1379(a).

72

stockholders the benefits of growth through the ownership of common stock. This can be important in a situation where corporate ownership is split between parents and children, with parents being given preferred stock, in order to give them fixed income, while leaving to the children the opportunities for growth in the investment over a longer period of time.

Even before the restrictions imposed by the Tax Reform Act of 1969, the use of Subchapter S corporations was by no means an unmixed blessing. Since the election to be taxed as a partnership had to be made at the beginning of the year, in many cases the opportunity had to be passed up because circumstances at the beginning of the year did not appear favorable to Subchapter S treatment. While getting out of Subchapter S is relatively easy, it does pose additional problems for the corporate shareholders and certainly requires careful consideration before adoption. For professional corporations, however, the limitation on contributions to retirement plans certainly makes the Subchapter S corporation far less attractive than it was prior to the Tax Reform Act of 1969.

5. How Do You Terminate the Subchapter S Election to Avoid the H.R. 10 Limits on Contributions?

Since the restrictions on Subchapter S corporations by the Tax Reform Act of 1969 make Subchapter S of dubious value, the question arises as to how the owners of a corporation may terminate the Subchapter S election and thereby get away from the H.R. 10 limitations on contributions to the retirement plans of the professional corporation.

One way to handle the problem would be to revoke the Subchapter S election within the first month of the taxable year of the corporation. A termination of the election will also automatically result from the issuance or transfer of stock to a shareholder who has not consented to the Subchapter S election. This also can result from the issuance of an additional class of stock, such as preferred.

A possible alternative to the termination of the Subchapter S election would be to amend the retirement plan of the corporation to provide that contributions on behalf of shareholder-employees will be reduced so that they cannot exceed the H.R. 10 limitations. In the event that the H.R. 10 limitations are at a later date alleviated or removed by Congress, then the corporation will not be denied Subchapter S treatment for a period of five years, which normally is the result where the Subchapter S election has been revoked.

I. What Are the Steps That Should Be Taken?

In order to make sure that all of the steps which should be taken in connection with the incorporation of the professional corporation are properly carried out, it will be desirable for those responsible to have a checklist of the steps that need to be taken. A checklist, setting forth each step, and perhaps allocating the responsibilities to the particular person directly responsible for carrying out the steps, will be very helpful and, in fact, necessary.

1. Who Is Responsible?

There will need to be a clear understanding as to just who is to be responsible for each particular step. Some of the steps will be primarily the responsibility of the attorney who is counsel for the corporation. The drafting of legal instruments will be his direct and primary responsibility. This will include not only the legal instruments involved in the incorporation, such as the Articles of Incorporation and By-laws, but also the employment agreements, the pension and profit-sharing plans, medical reimbursement plan and the bill of sale, leases and other legal instruments which may prove necessary to make sure that the corporation is properly organized and that property is properly transferred from the predecessor partnership to the corporation. The Certified Public Accountant will have primary responsibility for the various tax returns involved, as well as setting up the books of the corporation. Life insurance and other insurance policies will be the responsibility of the life and casualty underwriter. If there is a fixed-benefit pension plan involved, then the actuary will be very much concerned with that. The investment broker will be involved in the investment phase of the pension and profit-sharing plans and the bank, if a corporate trustee is selected for the retirement plans, and will also be involved with responsibilities in connection therewith.

In the case of a medical clinic which is organized as a professional corporation, if there are three or more doctors involved, then it is likely that a clinic manager will be in the picture. While the responsibility for operation of the corporation will be primarily that of the Board of Directors and the officers, in fact the clinic manager will generally carry out most of the steps which are the responsibility of the Board and of the officers.

2. How Will the Steps Be Communicated?

In allocating the responsibilities for the various steps to be carried out in connection with the incorporation and its implementation, numerous conferences between the shareholders of the corporation and counsel, as well as the Certified Public Accountant, will be generally involved. In many cases it will be helpful for the counsel to prepare a memorandum to the Board of Directors and officers setting forth in written form a checklist of the steps to be taken, and perhaps giving them an explanation of the significance of the particular steps, as well as the dates of performance of the particular steps involved. This will help to make sure that the organization of the corporation is properly handled and that the other steps incidental thereto, involved in the transfer of the properties, setting up of the employment agreements, retirement plans and various insurance programs, will be effectively and properly carried out.

3. What Are the Steps Necessary?

The steps involved in the organization of the corporation and implementation of the plan of incorporation fall into seven principal categories. Those categories involve the incorporation, which is the subject of Chapter 2; the transfer instruments, which are the subject of Chapter 3; the employment agreements, which are the subject of Chapter 4; the retirement plans, which are the subject of Chapter 5; the insurance agreements, which are the subject of Chapter 6 and certain miscellaneous steps which will round out the entire plan of incorporation and transfer of the professional business from the partnership or proprietorship to the corporation.

(a) *The Incorporation*

The incorporation of the enterprise involves 12 basic steps, all of which are primarily the concern of the counsel for the corporation. In carrying out these steps he will need the cooperation of the corporate officers and Board of Directors, as well as the Certified Public Accountant and, in the case of a medical clinic which incorporates, the clinic manager, as well.

How Do You Go About Organizing the Corporation?

The steps related to incorporation are as follows:

1. Draft Articles of Incorporation.
2. Draft By-laws.
3. Mail Articles of Incorporation with fee to Secretary of State.
4. Choose date to begin business as a corporation.
5. Order corporate record book, seal and certificates of stock.
6. Hold organizational meeting and elect officers and directors.
7. Provide corporation with corporate record book and seal.
8. Prepare organizational meeting minutes, including Section 1244 provision.
9. Issue stock certificates.
10. Prepare corporate resolution re bank accounts and open accounts.
11. Take steps to change to corporate name and notify creditors.
12. Change name on stationery and listings.

(b) *Transfer Instruments*

In connection with the transfer of property from the predecessor partnership or proprietorship to the corporation, there will be instruments which will be primarily the responsibility of counsel for the corporation. In addition, the Certified Public Accountant will be responsible for setting up the corporate books and records of the new corporation.

The steps to be taken in connection with the transfer of property to the corporation and the books and records are as follows:

1. Prepare bills of sale.
2. Prepare leases of real estate and equipment.
3. Set up corporate books and records.

(c) *Employment Agreements*

The new corporation will need to have employment agreements in writing prepared by the counsel for the corporation. This will help to establish the fact that the shareholder-employees are in fact employees of the corporation, and the duties and responsibilities of the shareholder-employees as employees will be clearly spelled out.

The steps that will need to be taken in connection with the employment agreements will be as follows:

How Do You Go About Organizing the Corporation?

1. Prepare Employment Agreement for shareholder-employees.
2. Have Employment Agreement signed.

(d) *The Retirement Plan*

The counsel for the corporation will need to prepare the various retirement plans for the corporation, whether they be pension plans, profit-sharing plans or thrift plans.

The steps to be taken in connection with such retirement plans will be as follows:

1. Prepare pension, profit-sharing plan and/or thrift plan.
2. Prepare notice of plans to employees.
3. File Form D-1 under Federal Welfare and Pension Disclosure Act if over 25 participants.
4. Prepare pension and profit-sharing booklet describing plan.
5. Submit pension or profit-sharing plan to IRS for approval on IRS Form 4573.

(e) *Insurance Policies*

The various insurance policies related to the different types of insurance to be purchased by the corporation will need to be considered by the counsel for the corporation, together with the life or casualty underwriter and the officers and Board of Directors. These instruments will include not only the insurance policies, but may also include a medical reimbursement plan, whether that is funded by insurance or not.

The steps to be taken in connection with the insurance and medical plans of the corporation are as follows:

1. Prepare medical expense reimbursement plan.
2. Transfer medical and hospitalization insurance.
3. Purchase disability insurance.
4. Purchase group life insurance.
5. Transfer malpractice insurance.
6. Transfer casualty insurance.

(f) *Tax Returns*

The proper organization of the professional corporation will involve the preparation and filing of various tax returns. These will be primarily the responsibility of the Certified Public Accountant, together with the corporate counsel and the officers and Board of Directors of the corporation.

The steps involved in connection with the tax returns will be as follows:

1. Prepare Application for Employer Identification Number on Form SS-4.
2. Make sure withholding is started as of date salaries are paid.
3. Prepare Unemployment Compensation forms.
4. Prepare State Sales Tax forms.
5. Meet franchise tax requirements.

(g) *Miscellaneous Steps*

In addition to the specific steps above discussed in connection with the incorporation, there will be a number of additional steps which will need to be taken to carry out the proper organization of the corporation. These will involve participation by the counsel for the corporation, the Certified Public Accountant, as well as corporate management, including the Board of Directors and the officers.

The miscellaneous steps which will be involved are as follows:

1. Select fiscal year of corporation.
2. Take out all special licenses.
3. Prepare Partnership Dissolution Agreement.
4. Terminate Keogh Plan.
5. Terminate partnership.
6. Furnish corporation management with list of procedural steps to be taken by the corporation.
7. Set up tickler system for review of all corporation matters about one month before end of first year.

While the above steps will generally cover most of the important instruments and procedures that will need to be carried out in order to organize and implement the organization of the corporation properly, in each individual case there will be additional steps that will need to be carried out properly, on time and in the correct sequence. The professional corporation will not operate itself, no more than it will set itself up. Individuals who are given the responsibility for performing each step will need to see that the steps are carried out. While it may seem to some of the shareholder-employees that many of these steps are mere technicalities, it is well to note that the corporation itself is a technical creature of the law and in order to be recognized and respected as a separate entity and person under the law, it will be essential that all of the steps involved be properly executed. Otherwise, the corporation may not be recognized as such and all of the effort that has gone into setting up the corporation may prove to have been in vain.

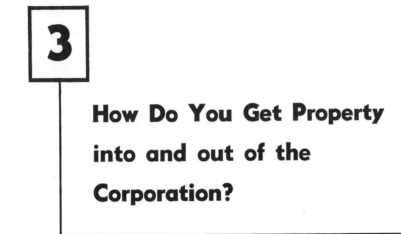

How Do You Get Property
into and out of the
Corporation?

Once the decision to incorporate is made and steps have been taken to form the corporation, the next question is one as to how the partnership gets property into the corporation and how the shareholder gets it out of the corporation. Several problems are involved. One deals with the question of tax-free transfer of property to a corporation at the time of incorporation. Others involve the question of how receivables and payables on the books of the partnership are to be handled, the manner of transfer of other property, the "bunching of income," where the partnership is on a fiscal year basis, the question of when to terminate the predecessor partnership, what needs to be done about goodwill and, finally, how does the shareholder get his property out of the corporation, either by sale or redemption of his stock, or by termination of the corporation itself.

A. How Do You Make the Transfer Tax-Free?

If it were not for Section 351 of the Internal Revenue Code, the exchange of the partnership property for stock of the corporation would be a taxable exchange. It would result in taxable income to the partners, measured by the difference between their basis in the partnership property on their books and the amount that they received in corporate stock. Generally, in an exchange, if what is received has a greater value than the property transferred, then the amount of the difference will be taxable as capital gain to the transferor. Section 351 provides relief from this tax if the transfer meets the express requirements of the Section. This requires that the transfer be made to the corporation "solely in exchange for stock or securities in such corporation." In addition, it requires that immediately after the exchange, the transferors must be "in control" of the corporation. Control is defined by the Internal Revenue Code as at least 80% of the total combined voting power of all classes of stock entitled to vote and at least 80% of the total number of shares of all other classes of stock of the corporation.[1] In the case of a professional corporation, the assets being transferred to the corporation by the predecessor partnership or proprietorship will be transferred to the corporation as in the case of an ordinary business. Section 351 expressly provides that stock or securities issued for services will not be considered as issued in return for property.

B. Should the Property Be Transferred by the Partnership or by the Partners Individually?

Until the issuance of Rev. Rul 70-239 [2] there was some question as to whether it would be better, in forming a professional corporation, to take over the property and business of a predecessor partnership, have the partnership transfer the assets to the corporation or, instead, have the partners liquidate the partnership and then individually transfer their shares of the property to the corporation for stock.

In Rev. Rul. 70-239 three different factual situations were presented: (1) The partnership transfers all of its assets, subject to its liabilities, to a new corporation for all of the stock. The partnership terminates and distributes the stock to its partners in proportion to their partnership interests. (2) The partnership terminates by distributing all of its assets,

---

[1] Sec. 368(c) of the Code.
[2] 1970-20 IRB, p. 15.

subject to its liabilities, to the partners in proportion to their partnership interests. Simultaneously, the partners transfer all of the property, subject to the liabilities, to the corporation in exchange for all of its stock. (3) The partners transfer their partnership interests to the corporation in exchange for all of the stock. This exchange terminates the partnership, and all of its assets, subject to its liabilities, become assets and liabilities of the corporation.

The ruling held that in all three situations Section 351 applied and no taxable gain or loss resulted from the transaction. It went on to state that the basis of the property acquired by the corporation was the same as its basis in the hands of the transferor partnership, and the basis of the stock received by each partner was an amount equal to the adjusted basis of his partnership interest. Accordingly, the ruling concluded that the transaction could be carried out in any of the three ways set forth in the ruling, each ending up with the same result. Where, however, there has been either appreciation or depreciation in the value of the property contributed to the corporation, the basis, both in the property held by the corporation, as well as in the stock of the shareholders, may differ, depending upon which of the three courses above discussed are followed. This can also happen where the partnership has purchased a partner's interest, which is likely to occur when a partner dies. Accordingly, before choosing between the three different alternative courses discussed above, it will be most important to consider which course will provide the best solution from the standpoint of determining the basis of the property in the hands of the corporation and the basis of each shareholder in his stock.[3]

C. What if the Liabilities Assumed by the Corporation Exceed the Basis of the Property Transferred to the Corporation?

A limitation on the tax-free effect of a Section 351 exchange arises by virtue of Section 357(c), where the amount of the liabilities assumed by the corporation exceeds the tax basis of the transferors in the property

---

[3] John S. Pennell and John C. O'Byrne, "Incorporating the Partnership—Federal Income Tax Considerations," 17 The Practical Lawyer, No. 2 (Feb. 1971), p. 51.

which was transferred to the corporation in exchange for its stock. Where the liability assumed by the corporation exceeds the transferor's basis in the property transferred, this will result in a taxable transaction to the extent of such excess. Similarly, under Section 357(b), if the principal purpose of the taxpayer with respect to the transaction is to avoid Federal income tax on the exchange, or, if his purpose was not a bona fide business purpose, then the exchange will be taxable, to the extent of the liability assumed.

In forming a professional corporation, it will, therefore, be necessary to make sure that the total amount of the liabilities assumed is compared against the total tax basis of the transferors in the property transferred in exchange for the corporate stock. If the liabilities are greater, then it will be necessary to pay off sufficient liabilities to make sure that the transaction is tax-free under Section 351. This is one of the many areas in which all of the parties involved will need to rely heavily on the accountant who is handling the books and tax returns for the partnership and the corporation.

D. How Do You Handle the Transfer of Accounts Receivable and Payable?

1. Accounts Receivable

Until recently those advising on the formation of professional corporations and associations had considerable qualms about transferring to the corporation or association the accounts receivable of the predecessor partnership. It was thought that the collection of the receivables by the corporation might give rise to a reallocation of the income back to the partnership on the ground that the income had been earned by the partners and not by the transferee corporation. Consequently, it was thought that the most conservative course and best, for that matter, would be to keep the partnership alive and have it collect and disburse to the partners the accounts receivable which had been earned by the partnership. This, of course, made necessary the keeping of two separate sets of books, one for the partnership and one for the corporation, and billing problems also were involved, as well as problems of upsetting the patients or clients of the professional entity involved.

The problem would appear to have been substantially resolved by a statement by the Chief Counsel of the Internal Revenue Service [4] to the effect that the accounts receivable will be taxed to the corporation and not to the partnership. An alternative would be to seek a ruling, but this would not now seem required, after the Chief Counsel's statement.

2. Accounts Payable

It would seem that the handling of accounts payable might very well differ from the handling of accounts receivable. This becomes quite important where a professional corporation is involved, since it will be likely that the liabilities assumed may well exceed the basis of the assets transferred because the accounts receivable, in a cash basis situation, will have a zero basis.[5] It was thought for some time that the accounts payable could not be transferred without some danger of having the deduction for the accounts payable denied to the corporation, since the corporation had not incurred the liabilities involved. It was also thought that the deduction would be denied to the partnership, since the partnership had not in fact paid the accounts. The statement of the Chief Counsel above referred to, however, indicated, on the basis that the basic policy of Section 351 is to treat the new corporation as a continuation of the previous business, that the new corporation should be regarded as standing in the shoes of the transferor, for purposes of taking tax deductions. Accordingly, the corporation should be allowed to deduct payments which the transferor could have deducted if he had continued to operate the business. Such a result is certainly clear if a ruling is obtained. A contrary result was reached in a recent Tax Court case, however.[6] Accordingly, payables probably should be paid by the transferor only.

E. What Do You Do About Transferring Other Property?

Where a partnership owns a clinic building, the problem arises, at the time of incorporation of the clinic, as to whether the building should be transferred to the new corporation. While the tax-free transfer of the

---

[4] Martin Worthy, "IRS Chief Counsel Outlines What Lies Ahead for Professional Corporations," 32 Jl. Taxation 88, 90 (1970).

[5] Raich v. Comm'r, 46 T.C. 604 (1966).

[6] Robert L. McCoy, T. C. Memo. 1971-34.

building to the corporation might seem logical at the time of incorporation, it should be borne in mind that loading up the corporation with a substantial amount of assets can present a problem later on to the new professional who gives consideration to becoming a shareholder. If the corporation has very substantial assets, then the purchase price of the stock in the corporation will be that much greater and could constitute a hurdle for the new professional when he tries to figure out how much he will have to put into the corporation when he joins it as a shareholder. Accordingly, a judgment decision must be made as to whether it might not be better to leave substantial assets out of the corporation altogether and have the corporation lease those assets from some other entity, such as the predecessor partnership, or a separate corporation which owns the real estate involved.

The same considerations apply to expensive equipment owned by the partnership; for example, equipment used in a medical specialty such as radiology or pathology. Some items, even though rather expensive, such as the library of a law office, nevertheless probably should be transferred to the corporation. In each case, the facts should be analyzed to determine whether it is best to leave the particular assets in another entity, with an arm's length lease to the professional corporation, or whether it would be satisfactory to transfer these particular assets to the professional corporation itself.

F. How Do You Solve the Problem of "Bunching of Income" in a Fiscal Year Partnership?

One of the most perplexing problems in forming professional corporations has been that of "bunching of income," when a partnership which is on a fiscal year basis seeks to transfer its assets to a professional corporation. The most extreme situation arises with a fiscal year partnership which has a fiscal year ending early in the year—for example, January 31. In that case, for each of the partners there is a problem of having to report in one taxable year income earned over a period of 23 months. This arises from the fact that the partnership's income for the fiscal year ending January 31 must be reported in its entirety, in the case of each partner, in his taxable calendar year in which January 31 falls. If the professional corporation is started in that same calendar year, then each of the professionals will be required to report also the salary and bonuses received by him during that same calendar year from the corporation.

This is not a situation peculiar to professional corporations alone. It always arises when a partnership which has been on a fiscal year basis is converted into a corporation. As a result, what had at one point in the past appeared to be a very helpful device to delay the reporting of earned income, now becomes a serious hurdle when the partners wish to change the form of their business from that of a partnership to a corporation.

What can be done about it? There is no panacea for this problem. About all that can be done is to try to straddle two taxable years of the individuals, by delaying some of the salaries from the corporation, so that they will be paid and reported in the next succeeding year of the corporation. If the income involved is subject to an extremely high bracket, it may be worthwhile for the individuals involved to seek some form of tax shelter for this particular year. Unfortunately, however, most tax shelters involve an investment over a period of more than one year, and often require a substantial capital investment, in addition to the deductible expense portion of the investment. The situation is one which requires careful study and some ingenuity, as well as possibly some financing by a bank in order to enable the individuals involved to defer some of their salary from the corporation, in order to shift it to the next taxable year. Once the 50% ceiling on earned income becomes applicable, as it will in 1972, the shift from a fiscal year partnership will be much less painful taxwise.

G. When Do You Terminate the Predecessor Partnership?

Whether the predecessor partnership should be terminated soon after the formation of the professional corporation depends upon the particular facts. It may well prove desirable to leave substantial assets in the partnership and to rent the property to the corporation. This would be true of a building or expensive equipment. It may well be that there are other business activities which have been operated in the partnership and which need not, or perhaps should not, be transferred to the professional corporation. By leaving the assets in the partnership, it makes it easier for a new professional to become a shareholder in the corporation, since the amount he will need to contribute to corporate capital for his stock will be that much less.

How Do You Get Property into and out of the Corporation?

H. Do You Transfer Goodwill to the Corporation?

1. Should Goodwill Be Valued as an Asset?

It will generally be desirable to consider that goodwill is not valued as an asset at the time of the formation of the corporation. This will eliminate some serious tax problems and should make it easier to avoid the "unreasonable compensation" question. In many professional situations, there is clearly no goodwill. For example, surgery is a branch of medicine where there can be little goodwill, if any at all. In a California case,[7] involving a divorce action, it was held that there was goodwill as community property. In that case, a physician had made $35,000 to $55,000 for the three years prior to his divorce. In dividing the community assets of $87,000, the court included $32,500 for the goodwill of the practice. The divorce decree awarded the goodwill to the husband but required him to make payments to his wife at the rate of $300 per month until she had received her half of the community assets, including the goodwill.

2. What Happens on the Sale of Stock Back to Corporation?

The founding shareholders, in many cases, may feel that they have a valuable right in the receivables, work-in-process and goodwill, separate and apart from the rights of the shareholders who come into the corporation later on. If, however, the founding shareholders insist that these items be considered in formulating the redemption agreement, they will be creating problems for later shareholders who may have to be dealing with those matters in the liquidation of the corporation. In such event, upon liquidation of the corporation the goodwill is subject to tax as ordinary income.

3. What Happens on Liquidation of the Corporation?

If receivables, work-in-process and goodwill have been considered in the basis for stock at the time of organization of the corporation, then the shareholders who have to handle the liquidation of the corporation will have to pay income tax on the collected receivables, because the shareholders have a basis in their stock, but not in their receivables. Any stock purchase plan which places high values on the corporate stock will re-

---

[7] Golden v. Golden, 75 Cal. Rep. 735 (1969).

quire large corporate earnings in order to provide the funds with which to pay the purchase price to the selling shareholder. In a 50% bracket, the payment of $75,000 for the purchase of the stock of a deceased shareholder will require that the corporation earn $150,000. The payment of the extra $75,000 will afford the surviving stockholders no tax benefit until they, in turn, terminate their employment. If they should die prior to retirement, the tax benefit would be lost to them entirely, because their shares would obtain a new tax basis, their fair market value, at the time of their death.

Any plan which serves to value the stock higher than need be will place a burden on the young professional who is interested in buying the stock. If, by any chance, the corporation proves to be a "collapsible" corporation,[8] then the gain to the seller on sale of his stock will be taxed at ordinary income tax rates, rather than on a capital gain basis: If the professional corporation has transferable goodwill as a result of giving accounts receivable, work-in-process and good will a value when the stock of the corporation is originally issued, then, even though the original incorporation was tax-free under Section 351, these particular assets may not escape taxation on liquidation. The cash-basis accounts receivable might cause the corporation to be considered "collapsible." This problem may be alleviated somewhat by planning the liquidation early in the stockholders' taxable year, because most of the receivables will be collected or proved worthless by the end of the stockholders' tax year. If liquidation of the corporation occurs late in the stockholder's year, however, then the stockholder may be taxed, not only on his cash-basis income for the year, but also on the value of the assets of this type distributed to him.

4. When Must Dividends Be Paid?

If a professional corporation can be said to have derived a substantial part of its income from goodwill, or from the operation of physical assets, such as a hospital, nursing home, or pharmacy, then the Internal Revenue Service might well contend that the portion of profits attributable to the goodwill or the physical assets should be disbursed to the shareholders in the form of a dividend, rather than as deductible compensation.

---

[8] Internal Revenue Code, Sec. 341.

How Do You Get Property into and out of the Corporation?

In the *Charles McCandless Tile Service* case,[9] the Court of Claims held that 15% of the net profits of the taxpayer-corporation, engaged in the tile business and owned by a father and son, represented a distribution of corporate earnings, rather than payment for services. Part of their salaries, the Court held, was, therefore, dividends. It is quite possible that the Internal Revenue Service might seek to apply the reasoning of that case to a professional corporation which makes a substantial portion of its profit from the use of its capital, rather than from the personal services of the shareholder employees.

Another similar case [10] involved a Circuit Court of Appeals decision in connection with a printing company. The owner established his own salary and commissions, as well as the contribution to the corporation's profit-sharing plan. The total compensation paid to him consisted of almost 60% of the corporation's distributable income. No dividends were paid during this period. The Court held that part of what he had treated as compensation was, in fact, a dividend on the corporate assets, rather than compensation.

Another case that will need to be kept in mind in connection with the dividend question where a professional corporation is organized was recently decided by the Tax Court.[11] In that case, the taxpayer was both the president and only stockholder actively engaged in operating the corporation. He owned approximately 43% of the stock and his father-in-law owned a similar amount. During the years in question, the taxpayer withdrew from the corporation amounts in excess of his salary. He paid no interest on such amounts and did not execute any note or give any security. It appeared that there was no realistic means of repayment of the amount to the corporation, nor was any time set for repayment. During the period in question, the corporation did not declare or pay any dividends on its stock. The Tax Court held that under such circumstances, the distributions were taxable to the president of the corporation as dividends.

In light of these three cases, it appears that in organizing a professional corporation, it will be important to bear in mind that distributions from the corporation, while ostensibly set up as salaries for services, or as

---

[9] 422 F.2d 1336 (Ct. Cl. 1970).
[10] Barton-Gillet Co. v. Comm'r,—F.2d—(CA4, 6/11/71) affirming 29 TCM 679 (1970).
[11] Carl G. Braun et al, TC Memo 1971-144.

some other form of compensation, or as loans, may, nevertheless, be considered by the Service and the courts to constitute dividends, rather than deductible compensation or loans.

5. How Can the Dividends Problem Be Solved?

Because of the danger that the Courts will consider that part of the compensation of the shareholder-employees of a professional corporation may represent earnings on assets of the corporation, it will be advisable generally to keep the assets of the corporation as low as possible. For that reason, it will be desirable to attribute little, if any, value to goodwill at the time the corporation is organized. If the founding shareholders believe that they should be paid something for their goodwill and work-in-process, then it would seem desirable to take that into account in setting up their compensation agreements, rather than attributing any value to goodwill at the time of transfer of the partnership assets to the newly organized professional corporation.

The ultimate scope of the *McCandless* holding still remains to be seen. By holding that where salaries paid are in the same proportion as the ownership of the stock, the amount paid as salaries may, in fact, be considered in part to be a payment of dividends, the decision seems to eliminate the right that a corporation has to accumulate earnings, at least until those earnings have reached the total amount of $100,000, since the Internal Revenue Code does not consider accumulated earnings unreasonable until they have passed that figure.[12] Certainly the total amount of capital involved in the corporation will be an important factor. If there is not very much capital, then a reasonable return on that capital, in the form of dividends, rather than compensation, would not produce as substantial a percentage as the 15% set by the Court in the *McCandless* decision. Certainly that decision warrants careful consideration at the time of organization of the professional corporation. It would appear wise, in the light of the decision, to not include goodwill as an asset of the partnership to be transferred to the corporation. It would also seem well to bear in mind that the Service, in examining the tax returns of a professional corporation and its shareholders, will be inclined to consider the entire situation in the

---

[12] Internal Revenue Code, Sec. 531.

How Do You Get Property into and out of the Corporation?

light of the *McCandless* holding and its possible application to the particular set of facts involved.

I. How Do You Get Out of the Corporation?

Terminating a professional corporation and getting property out of it presents a number of problems. It must be borne in mind that the entity is not a partnership, and getting out or terminating the corporation is not the same as terminating the partnership.

1. How Does One Shareholder Get Out?

The problem of a single shareholder getting out is, of course, different from that of termination of the corporation. If the shareholder sells his stock to another shareholder or to a new shareholder, then his tax problems are simple, since, if the amount he receives is greater than his basis in the stock, he has capital gain.

Sometimes there may be more than one member of the family who is a stockholder—for example, a father and son. In such event the stock attribution rules will apply [13] so that the redemption might very well be treated as a redemption which is essentially equivalent to a dividend.[14]

Where the problem is one of a single shareholder trying to dispose of his stock, it would appear that in planning the corporation and its operations, it would be wise to make sure that the amount invested in the stock is kept at the lowest possible level. The corporation should not retain earnings, but it should pay them out in the form of compensation and other benefits to employees, both shareholder and non-shareholder. The shareholder-employee should look primarily to his compensation and to his fringe benefits, rather than to what he might receive at the time of sale of his stock, or upon termination or liquidation of the corporation itself. The problems involved in the redemption of stock, as well as the problems on termination or liquidation of the corporation, can be minimized by making sure that the corporation does not build up its capital or surplus any more than is absolutely necessary. In other words, do not try to make the corporation "an incorporated pocketbook," or even a long-term capital

---

[13] Internal Revenue Code, Sec. 318.
[14] Internal Revenue Code, Sec. 302(b).

92

gain investment. A shareholder-employee should be content to receive his benefits in the form of ordinary income, to the extent of his compensation, and tax deductible fringe benefits purchased for him by the corporation and free of tax to him, at least at the time of purchase of those benefits by the corporation.

2. Liquidation or Termination of the Corporation

Liquidation of a corporation may be accomplished without a double tax, by bringing about the liquidation within a period of one month under Section 333 of the Code, or within 12 months under Section 337.

(a) *One-Month Liquidation*

Where a corporation is liquidated within a period of one calendar month, the gain to the shareholders will be recognized only to the extent of the greater of the assets received in the form of money, or of stock or securities, on the one hand, or of accumulated earnings, on the other. The liquidation must be effected through a plan of liquidation.

(b) *12-Month Liquidation*

The more customary type of complete liquidation is the 12-month liquidation. This must be effected through a plan of liquidation which will generally be included in the minutes of the corporation. By making the liquidation comply with the statutory provisions, the possible double tax, once to the corporation and again to the shareholder, is eliminated. Nevertheless, there may be problems as to whether the tax to the shareholder is all in the form of capital gain or whether part of it must be considered ordinary income. Where some of the corporate assets consist of receivables, then they may very well be taxed to the corporation. Moreover, if the property distributed to the shareholder on liquidation is subject to a liability which exceeds the corporation's basis in such property, there may be a taxable gain to the corporation. Similarly, there may be tax to the corporation on recaptured depreciation.

Perhaps the most important simple and basic rule for a professional corporation, in order to avoid problems on termination and liquidation of the corporation, or on redemption or sale of a stockholders' shares, is to keep to a minimum the accumulations of corporate earnings. This can be done by paying out the maximum amount to the shareholder-employee as compensation and by making substantial contributions to the retirement plans and other tax-deductible payments for the benefit of employees.

3. What About Termination of the One-Man Corporation?

Where the corporation is a one-man corporation, there will be special problems, since the question arises as to what happens to the corporation. In California, the corporation becomes an ordinary corporation when the sole stockholder dies. Where continuation of the entity in the form of an ordinary corporation is not provided for by state statute, then it would appear that whatever assets there are in the corporation, subject to the liabilities, belong to the sole stockholder's estate and will pass as provided by his will or by intestacy. In a few states, such as Texas, there is provision for a one-man association. In some cases a "nominee" associate, owning a small number of shares, has been brought in, generally on a reciprocal basis. Where the state law in question is an association statute, rather than a corporation statute, then even with the two-man association a practical problem arises on the death of one of the associates, since then the entity presumably becomes a one-man association. Problems exist on the death of the sole associate, as in the case of the death of a sole stockholder of a professional corporation. May the estate of the deceased associate continue to own an interest in the association? This would appear to be a question to which there is no complete answer as yet, although any ownership of stock by anyone who is not licensed by the state to practice the particular profession will certainly not be permitted for any substantial length of time. Ownership by an estate would certainly be permitted for as long as was reasonably required to take care of the necessities of transfer at death.

A further problem in the case of the one-man association is whether, despite a state statute providing therefor, a one-man association will be recognized as a corporation by the Internal Revenue Service. The question, to some extent, involves a problem of semantics. How can one man associate with himself? If a solution to this is sought by making another member of the same profession a nominal associate, by giving him perhaps a 5% interest, will this make it a valid association? Can it be attacked on the basis that it is a sham and therefore should be treated as in fact a one-man association? This will, of course, bring in additional problems with respect to the personal holding company question, assignment of income and "sham" corporation questions, all of which are discussed at length in Chapter 7.

In the case of at least one field office in Texas, where, as in a number of states, the state statute provides for a one-man association, the field office held at one point that a favorable determination letter would not be issued on a pension or profit-sharing plan where there was only one associate who was employed full time, regardless of the fact that there might be a number of other associates who actually owned an interest in the association. In other words, the "nominal" associate, who owns only a small interest in the association and does not actually work full time for the association, would not be recognized as an associate.

The Internal Revenue Service has now ruled informally, by verbal ruling only, that a one-man association, under the Texas Professional Association Act, will be recognized. This position would, of course, appear to take care of the one-man association question in the other states where the state statute provides for one-man professional associations. It will, of course, be very important for those forming one-man associations to check carefully with the field offices in the particular state involved to make sure that the particular field office will, in fact, issue a determination letter with respect to the one-man association, since there has not been any written ruling from the Service as yet to give complete assurance on this matter. It would seem, however, that in time the Service should rule on this question in writing, so that those interested in forming one-man associations would receive the same treatment under the Federal tax laws as those forming one-man corporations.

4

How Do You Handle

Compensation?

Once the corporation has been established and the problems of transferring property and accounts receivable have been dealt with, the next question that arises is that of compensation to the shareholders for their services. How is that handled? As partners, they have been accustomed to having a drawing account, perhaps in a modest sum each month, and with a distribution of profits, perhaps quarterly, and then a final distribution of profits at the end of the year. Their living patterns have been geared to that type of a cash flow into their individual bank accounts and, to the extent that it can be accomplished, they generally would prefer that the pattern be continued as far as possible without destroying the validity of the corporation for tax purposes. Nevertheless, since it is a corporation we are now dealing with, the former partners, who are now shareholders, must consider themselves employees of a corporation and their compensation arrangements must be handled in that light. This means that instead of a drawing account and sharing of profits, the professionals are now shareholder-employees and will receive salaries on a regular monthly basis, with a bonus which will supplement the salaries. In the case of the partnership, the drawing accounts often are modest in amount and may not constitute a major portion of the total compensation of the partners for the year. As employees of a corporation, however, it will be essential to establish salaries which will constitute the principal portion of the employees' compensation during the year, with the bonus constituting basically a lesser amount as supplementary compensation in addition to the salary.

A. How Are the Employment Agreements Prepared?

The employment agreement will set forth the salary and bonus arrangement for the shareholder-employee. While a written employment agreement may not be needed in the case of employees other than shareholders, the shareholder-employees definitely need a written agreement which clearly sets forth their salaries and the basis on which the bonus will be computed.

1. How Should Salaries Be Determined?

As in the case of ordinary corporations, the determination of salaries will be made by the Board of Directors, possibly upon the recommendation of the executive committee. In determining salaries, it is essential to consider what will be done about other methods of remuneration, such as bonuses, and what will be the contribution to qualified pension and profit-sharing plans and for other fringe benefits. Since a first-class plan, involving a pension and profit-sharing plan, together with the other fringe benefits, will often cost as much as 20% of an employee's total compensation, there will generally need to be an evaluation of the costs of all those other benefits, and a buffer of perhaps 5%, so that salaries, which need to be fixed in amount, can be determined with reasonable accuracy. While it will be possible to pay salaries on a partial basis, or skip them altogether for some periods of time; nevertheless, they need to be reasonably certain in amount in order to give the salary arrangement the necessary corporate attributes, and the former partners will be acting and be paid as corporate employees.

(a) May They Be Based on Production?

In dealing with professional people, salaries based on production certainly make sense. Depending upon the profession, the salaries may be based in part upon work done and in part upon credit for work obtained. Other criteria, such as reputation and professional image for the enterprise, may also be considered. What about compensation to a particular employee in excess of his billings? Some concern has been expressed by a number of writers as to the problems of a senior law firm member, who may have been accustomed to receiving compensation far in excess of his billings or production. The determination of the value of the services of a particular professional must be left to the Board of Directors, in the last analysis, since they presumably are the most competent to determine exactly what salaries should be paid to each professional employed by the enterprise.

(b) *How Do They Relate to Prior Earnings of Partners?*

Since the package of benefits provided by a pension and profit-sharing plan, together with group life insurance, disability insurance, medical reimbursement and hospitalization insurance, will often aggregate as much as 20% of total compensation, it would seem that in setting salaries for professionals in a new professional corporation it would be well to look toward a salary of approximately 75% of their compensation in the predecessor partnership. This would allow for 20% for all of the fringe benefits, including the pension and profit-sharing plans, and a 5% buffer, in the form of a bonus, to be paid quarterly, semi-annually or annually. The bonus serves to adjust the compensation to the changes in overall income of the enterprise; whereas, the salary and the various fringe benefits would be considerably more fixed.

In setting salaries initially, the compensation previously drawn by the partners, including bonuses, would be a good place to start. Then, after a determination of how much the fringe benefits would cost, the salaries would be set in light thereof, with perhaps 5% of prior compensation to serve as the buffer, this amount to be reflected at the end of the year in the form of the bonus to the shareholder-employees.

2. How Do You Determine Bonuses?

In determining bonuses, certainly changes in billings or production will be a major factor. By and large, salaries probably should not be changed more often than annually, so that as a younger man moves up in his earnings, this will be reflected each year in his bonus, and only in the following year in terms of salary increase.

The method of determining salaries and bonuses, involving allocation between departments in a large professional group, is not very different from that which has to be employed in the case of a large partnership. Large medical clinics and law firms are broken down into various departments. In such large professional entities, compensation in the form of salaries and bonuses will often be determined partly on the basis of individual performance and partly on the basis of departmental performance or profit.

(a) *How Much Latitude Is There for Discretion?*

Once the major question of whether the professional corporation is properly a corporation under state law has been determined, it would seem that latitude in determining bonuses is about as broad with professional corporations as it is with ordinary business corporations. The Board of Directors has the authority to determine the bonuses. As long as it proceeds in a fashion acceptable to the shareholders, there would seem to be little cause to quarrel with the Board's determination. The test of reasonableness, of course, has to be kept in mind.

(b) *How Do Bonuses Relate to Fixed Salary?*

In determining the relationship of bonuses to salary, a major factor would seem to be the need for money at regular intervals on the part of the shareholder-employees. In a partnership this is determined to some extent by the relationship of withdrawals to bonuses. In a corporation there will need to be a bonus in addition to salary, so that some flexibility for compensation may be provided. This will not only take care of variations in the success of the entire enterprise, but also will accommodate changes that may be occurring as between shareholder-employees. Some of them may be going up on the compensation scale and others may be headed in the other direction. In the case of a professional corporation, the Board of Directors has a substantial responsibility in the determination of salaries and bonuses and certainly mutual good faith and confidence is required.

3. What Should the Employment Agreement Provide?

The agreement should cover virtually all of the provisions which are normally found in a partnership agreement. This would include such matters as duties, furnishing of facilities, compensation, vacations, arrangements for illness and disability, death benefits, restrictions against competition and, possibly, deferred compensation. In a medical practice, the covenant not to compete is often of little value and may, in fact, create problems at a time of withdrawal or dissolution which make its inclusion in the employment agreement dubious at best.

How Do You Handle Compensation?

Generally, the employment agreement will provide for restrictions on outside activities of the professional employee. It will require that he maintain a good standing in his profession and will set forth the basis upon which his employment may be terminated. Among other matters that may well be included will be the relationship to his compensation of expenses which he may incur in the performance of his duties. This will include expenses for automobiles, entertainment and attendance at various functions required in the course of the performance of his duties, as well as what will be done as to professional dues.

The agreement should provide what happens to the professional records and files if the employee leaves. The American Medical Association and American Bar Association canons provide that the patient or client has the right to control them.

Among the most important provisions will be those relating to the question of benefits upon termination of employment, upon four different contingencies: (1) retirement, (2) disability, (3) death, (4) termination due to some other cause. These four contingencies will generally be provided for by a number of the fringe benefits purchased with the 20% of a shareholder-employee's prior earnings as a partner, discussed previously. His retirement can be provided for through the pension plan of the corporation. His disability can be provided for through disability insurance purchased by the corporation and, at a later point, taken up by the pension plan, in case of permanent and total disability. The shareholder-employee's death will be provided for through group life insurance and possibly insurance purchased by the pension trust, as well as by key-man insurance to fund the stock purchase agreement. The possibility of the man's having to quit or getting fired may be protected against by contributions to the corporation's profit-sharing or thrift plan. This provides a means of saving for a rainy day, or for large capital commitments. Each of these forms of benefits should be considered as it ties in with the employment contract.

B. What Is Unreasonable Compensation?

The most serious problem arising with respect to the compensation question is that relating to unreasonableness. How can the Board of Directors determine what compensation is reasonable? The answer involves all of the factors which must be considered in the case of compensation to ordinary corporate executives, but it also includes additional factors which are peculiar to professional people.

1. What Determines Reasonableness for a Professional Employee?

To determine whether compensation is reasonable for a professional employee, all of the payments to him or on his behalf will need to be considered. This will include not only salaries and bonuses, but also contributions to pension and profit-sharing plans, group life insurance, medical reimbursement plans and disability and hospitalization insurance payments. The section of the Code we are dealing with is Section 162(a), relating to trade or business expenses. In addition, Section 212, relating to expenses incurred for the production of income, may also come into play.

Since the personal services of the professional produce the income of the professional corporation, it can be argued that whatever is paid the professional for his services by a professional corporation will be clearly reasonable, because he earned all of the income. This would appear to be true, even in the case of unusually large fees which might be obtained by lawyers in a very successful case—perhaps, in some respects, even a windfall.

If a deduction for the compensation to the professional shareholder-employee is disallowed as being unreasonable, it would seem that the disallowance would be apportioned among the component parts of his compensation; that is, salary, bonuses and contributions for the purchase of his fringe benefits.

Where bonuses are paid to shareholder-employees for the purpose of siphoning off corporate profits, rather than as compensation for services, they will be disallowed. In one case,[1] the Tax Court held that a substantial part of bonuses paid by three stockholders of a drug store corporation to themselves, in addition to salaries, constituted unreasonable compensation, since the bonuses were merely a device for paying out to the shareholders the rest of the profits over and above basic salaries. In that case, 90% of the profits of the business was paid in the form of bonuses and the bonuses were paid in proportion to stockholdings. The bonuses represented, in the case of one stockholder, two-thirds of his compensation for the year.

---

[1] Craig's Drug Store, Inc. v. Comm'r, 28 TCM 1104 (1969).

How Do You Handle Compensation?

2. How Is It Affected by Income Attributable to the Use of Property?

In the case of some professional corporation statutes, the corporation is permitted to invest in stocks, bonds and other investments. Where some of the income is derived from such investments, it will be possible for the Internal Revenue Service to contend that, to the extent that the profits from the investments contributed to the total corporate profits, the compensation will be unreasonable. This points to the question of what is a reasonable return on capital.

In the leading case on this point, the *Klamath Medical Bureau case,*[2] the amount paid to doctors in a professional corporation that also supplied hospital facilities exceeded the amount of their personal billings for medical services. The Tax Court in that case held that the salaries were reasonable only in the amount of the doctors' net billings. Payments in excess of those amounts were held to be unreasonable and non-deductible to the corporation.

In another case on this point,[3] a similar holding was made by the Tax Court where an elderly and relatively inactive doctor and his two sons owned all of the stock of an incorporated hospital. The elderly doctor, who devoted only part of his time to his services to the hospital, received 5% of the gross receipts of the corporation. The two sons were paid their entire billings, although one son received more than his individual billings and the other received less. Other doctors who were not shareholders received only 60% of the fees attributable to their services. The Tax Court held that the compensation to the older doctor was unreasonable to the extent that it exceeded $100 per week. It permitted a deduction for the full amount paid to the two sons. The Court rejected the contention that the test of 100% of billings should be applied to the individual doctors, rather than to their aggregate billings.

In light of the two Tax Court cases discussed above, it appears that in determining the compensation of shareholder-employees it will be important to see how their pay relates to the amount of their billings.

---

[2] Klamath Medical Service Bureau v. Comm'r, 261 F.2d 842 (CA 9, 1958).
[3] McClung Hospital, Inc., 19 TCM 449 (1960).

How Do You Handle Compensation?

3. How Is Reasonableness Affected by Contributions to Qualified Retirement Plans?

In adopting retirement plans, it will generally be desirable for the Board of Directors to take into account the fact that, as between older and younger shareholder-employees, a pension plan is more likely to be of greater immediate benefit to the older than to the younger. Moreover, the younger ones are likely to have much more pressing cash needs. Consequently, it may be that salary and bonus adjustments should be made to take these factors into account and salaries for the older employees might very well be considerably less, in the case of the professional corporation, because the purchase of their pension benefits costs much more than it does for the younger ones. The younger employees, with children to educate and mortgages to pay, perhaps cannot afford a reduction in their regular compensation as readily as can the older ones. It may also be that in the first year or two of the corporation, the level of payments to the pension and profit-sharing plans might well be less than those which are the main objective. A period of two or three years of adjustment will generally be helpful. A profit-sharing or savings plan might very well be started at the beginning of the first year of the corporation; whereas, the pension plan perhaps should not be adopted until near the end of the first taxable year, and perhaps not in full force until perhaps the second or third year. Fringe benefits, such as group life insurance, disability insurance, medical reimbursement and hospitalization, generally should be started as soon as the corporation is organized.

4. What About Payments to Retired Partners?

In the case of some professional corporations, there will be a problem presented by an arrangement under which the predecessor partnership has been paying the retired partners, although they were no longer rendering services to the partnership. May the corporation take on this responsibility and deduct any amounts paid to the retired partners? The deductibility of such amounts would appear to be dubious, since the partners who had been retired prior to the formation of the corporation certainly could not be said to have rendered any services to the corporation itself. Perhaps the blanket of approval given to the transfer of accounts receivable and payable to the new corporation might, perhaps, be extended to cover these payments to the retired partners,[4] but it would appear to be better for the partnership to take care of these payments in some fashion prior to the transfer of the professional operations and assets to the professional corporation.

5. Should the Employment Agreement Provide for the Return of Compensation Held to Be Excessive?

The Tax Court has held [5] that where the by-laws of a corporation at the time of its incorporation required that any part of an officer's salary which was disallowed as a deduction for income tax purposes should be repaid to the corporation and part of the salary was repaid, the repayment was deductible in the year repaid. Would such a provision direct the attention of the Service to the question of the reasonableness of the compensation? The Service has recently ruled [6] that the voluntary return of wages to a corporation by an officer does not affect the Social Security taxes involved. This would seem, perhaps, to imply that it does relieve him of income tax on such wages. One must also consider whether some of the shareholder-employees might not feel that once they have been paid compensation, in accordance with their employment agreement, they should not be required to repay it to the corporation.

6. What About Unreasonable Compensation in the Case of a One-Man Corporation?

The question of reasonableness of compensation in the case of a one-man corporation would appear to have few ground rules. In the case of a professional shareholder-employee, it would appear that he could, in good conscience, assert that whatever the corporation earned was earned by virtue of his personal services. This certainly would appear to be true unless there was a substantial amount of property involved in rendering the service. For example, in the case of a pathologist or radiologist, if a large amount of very expensive equipment was owned by the professional corporation itself, then it might be contended by the Service that part of the profit of the corporation was attributable to the expensive equipment

---

[4] See n. 3, Chapter 3.
[5] Vincent E. Oswald, 49 TC 745 (1968).
[6] Rev. Rul. 3121, 1971-27 I.R.B. 24.

used in rendering the services and, therefore, some reasonable allocation of profit should be made to the expensive equipment. The question of when property of an enterprise is a "material income-producing factor" has often been considered in the tax area and it would appear that in the case of a one-man corporation, as in the case of corporations with more than one shareholder, the question gets down to one of facts. If, as discussed previously in Paragraph 2, the property involved contributes substantially to the corporate profit, than certainly it may well be contended by the Service that such profit as is attributable to the property used in the business should not be paid to the shareholder-employee as part of his compensation.

7. What Factors Determine Reasonableness of Compensation?

In determining the question of reasonableness of compensation, the Courts have generally discussed a number of different factors. No one of them appears ever to be controlling, and about the only conclusion that can be drawn from the cases is that it will depend upon the facts involved in the particular case. Among the factors which have been considered by the Courts are those relating to the quality and quantity of service performed by the employee, the corporate history with respect to compensation and dividends, the relationship of the compensation to corporate income and the shareholdings of the employees, as well as the question of how does the compensation paid by this corporation compare to compensation paid by other corporations, similarly situated, to employees performing similar services.

It might be helpful to list 12 of the most frequently considered factors which, under the cases, appear to have influenced the decision of reasonableness of compensation. These factors certainly are not all-exclusive and they are often intertwined and commingled in the particular factual conditions involved in a particular case. Nevertheless, it should prove helpful to consider these factors in light of all the facts in each case to see whether they apply, and if so, what weight should be given to each of them.

(1) *What Is the Quality of Service Rendered by the Employee?* In this regard not only will his general qualifications be considered, but also any special qualification which warrants particularly special compensation. An example of this would be

the services of a surgeon who has perfected a particular type of operation or a lawyer who has developed special skill in an extremely complicated and difficult area of the law. As an illustration of this, in a case involving a corporate executive who was also an inventor, the Tax Court upheld the reasonableness of almost $290,000 per year, for the reason that the president of the corporation was, in addition to being chief executive of the corporation, an inventor of electrical equipment and the holder of many patents thereon.[7]

(2) *What Is the Employee's Professional Background?* Included in this factor would be the extent and nature of his education, training and experience. This would include not only his formal education, but also any special training and experience that entered into his capacity for the performance of high-caliber work. In the case of a professional employee, this would include the various degrees that he had earned, as well as his recognition in his professional field, including, for example, the publication of professional books and articles.

(3) *What Is the Difficulty of the Work Involved?* Where the work performed by the particular employee is of a particularly difficult nature, as, for example, certain operations performed by a surgeon, then this should enter into the question of reasonableness. Where an attorney, for example, achieved a particularly profitable result on a contingent basis, this might well justify much higher compensation than would the performance of capable work where there was not a high degree of difficulty involved in achieving a particular result.

(4) *What Is the Amount of Responsibility Assumed?* Where the employee takes on a high degree of responsibility, this can also affect the question of reasonableness of his compensation. This might be involved in the building of a skyscraper on the basis of the work of an architect, or putting together the legal basis for an involved corporate reorganization or some other type of difficult legal matter, in the case of a lawyer.

(5) *How Much of His Time Does the Employee Devote to His*

---

[7] Appleton Electric Co. v. Comm'r, 26 TCM 1043 (1967).

How Do You Handle Compensation?

Work? This question will involve the quantity of the employee's work. Does he devote all of his time to the job or does he only devote part of it? In some cases the length of the working day or of the working week might well affect the reasonableness of the compensation involved.

(6) *How Do the Payments of Compensation Relate to Compensation Paid in Prior Years?* If the compensation in question is substantially in line with compensation in prior years, this would tend to indicate reasonableness. The fact that compensation in prior years might have been considerably less than would ordinarily be considered reasonable might well justify higher compensation in the current year because the particular employee had been substantially underpaid for prior years.

(7) *What Is the Corporate Policy with Respect to Compensation to All of Its Employees?* The amounts paid to the other employees of the corporation can provide some comparative test to apply to the compensation paid to the particular employee involved, since the compensation paid to other employees will provide a possible measuring stick, although not by itself be conclusive.

(8) *What Dividends Have Been Paid?* If dividends have been paid in the past, as well as in the current year, then it may well be that a reasonable return to the shareholders on their stock has been reflected in the dividends. If no dividends have been paid in the past and none are paid in the current year, then, if property is a substantial income-producing factor, perhaps, to some extent, the compensation might be attacked on the ground that it represents, at least in part, return on capital rather than compensation for services.

(9) *How Does the Compensation to the Employee Relate to the Gross and the Net Income of the Corporation?* If the compensation to the particular employee is very large, when compared to the gross and the net income of the corporation, this might be said to reflect on the reasonableness of the compensation in some situations. Where, however, as in the case of a professional corporation, the income of the corporation is derived

primarily, if not exclusively, from the services of the share-holder-employees, this factor will not be of great importance, even though in the case of corporations generally it can be a matter of some importance in determining reasonableness of compensation.

(10) *How Does the Compensation of the Shareholder-Employees Relate to Their Percentage of Shareholdings?* If the compensation paid to the shareholder-employees is indirectly related, percentagewise, to their holdings of corporate stock, then this fact can be pointed to by the Service as an indication that the compensation is, at least in part, really a dividend rather than compensation for services performed. The closer the relationship, in terms of percentages, the more telling will be the argument for the Service.

(11) *What Is the Relationship of the Compensation to the Year-End Profit of the Corporation?* Where the compensation has been paid to the shareholder-employee particularly in the form of a bonus at year end, if the bonus is large in relation to the year-end profit of the corporation, the Service may claim that the bonus was paid to clean out the corporate till, so that there would be no profit to be taxed to the corporation. In the case of a professional corporation, where the profit is derived largely, if not entirely, from the professional services of the shareholder-employees, this argument would seem to be of less importance than in the case of the ordinary corporation.

(12) *How Does the Compensation Paid to the Shareholder-Employees Compare with the Compensation Paid to Similar Employees of Other Corporations in the Same Line of Business?* In the case of compensation to corporate executives generally, this test is of considerable importance, as a rule. In the case of professional corporations, however, comparisons between corporations may be more difficult to sustain, since the nature of professional services is such that, for the most part, whatever a professional is able to command in the marketplace appears to be the best test of what his services are worth. If the general public, free to choose among professionals, selects a particular professional corporation to render those services, it

appears that the public has made the decision as to what those services are worth. What other professional corporations might pay their shareholder-employees for similar services would not appear to be nearly as important as comparative compensation paid to executives in industry generally.

The above factors will provide some tests to apply in a given situation, but in the last analysis, the judgment of the Board of Directors of the corporation will have to be given considerable weight. The Service may use any or all of these tests to base its case of unreasonableness. For this reason, it will be well to bear all of them in mind when setting salaries and bonuses, as well as other types of benefits to the shareholder-employees of the professional corporation.

C. Deferred Compensation—What Can Be Done Through Deferred Compensation Agreements?

While deferred compensation agreements are fairly routine for ordinary corporations, the use of deferred compensation contracts for professional corporations would appear to be doubtful at best. In the case of professional partnerships, it is fairly customary to provide for some form of deferred compensation to retiring partners, and this gives the continuing, active partners a deduction for the amounts paid to the retiring partner. The retiring partner, since his income has been generally reduced as to amount, may well be in a lower bracket than his fellow partners, so that, from a tax standpoint, the arrangement may prove advantageous to all concerned. In the case of a professional corporation, however, the use of a deferred compensation agreement probably would bring more complications taxwise than it would benefits. It would seem wiser to handle the compensation situation through salary, bonus and contributions to various types of retirement plans, as well as deductible insurance, rather than introducing the more sophisticated and complicated procedures involved in a deferred compensation agreement. Section 1348 of the Code, added by the Tax Reform Act of 1969, and providing for the 50% maximum tax on earned income, expressly states that it does not apply to deferred compensation.

In the case of a professional corporation where there are some shareholder-employees who are close to retirement and where provision for their retirement through a pension plan is not feasible, a deferred compensation agreement might prove a desirable solution, since it will provide a means, substantially as in the case of the partnership, to give these particular shareholder-employees compensation over a period of years, with such compensation deductible to the corporation and, in effect, to the other shareholder-employees.

D. How Do You Handle Expenses?

1. What About Cars and Travel Expense?

Generally, a professional shareholder-employee will need to have some use of an automobile in connection with the rendering of his services. Of course it is clear that a professional is not permitted to deduct the cost of commuting between his home and his place of business. Some professionals seem to have the idea that the formation of a professional corporation makes car and travel expenses deductible, which might not otherwise be so. This certainly is not true. The travel and car expense must be justified on the basis of the particular facts in each situation. Where mileage is the basis on which car expense is to be sought, the Internal Revenue Service now permits a 12 cents per mile deduction. The taxpayer may, however, by keeping track of his exact expenses, perhaps deduct more than that on the basis of the miles driven. In order to do so, he must keep proper and adequate records. Travel expenses of all kinds which are necessary to the performance of the services of the shareholder-employee certainly may, as reasonable and necessary expenses of the corporation in doing business, be deducted.

2. What About Entertainment Expense?

Reasonable and necessary entertainment, which contributes to the production of income, certainly is a justifiable deduction under the Internal Revenue Code. The problems get down mainly to one of keeping adequate and proper records in accordance with the rulings of the Internal Revenue Service.[8]

---

[8] Internal Revenue Code, Sec. 274.

3. How Do You Handle Professional Dues?

The payment of professional dues is certainly a necessary and justifiable expense of a professional corporation. There may be items in the twilight zone which might be justified on either the dues or entertainment basis. Certainly adequate and complete records, kept in accordance with the Internal Revenue Service requirements, are necessary. It must be noted, however, that just because the entity involved is a corporation does not in any way make deductible expenses which would not otherwise be deductible by a partnership or proprietorship.

E. What About Payments of Compensation to Widows?

The question of compensation by a corporation to the widow of an employee has been litigated over a period of many years. In most cases, the payment has been made as a posthumous recognition of the decedent's services to the corporation, or out of concern for the economic plight of the widow. In most situations, the $5,000 death benefit provided by Section 101(b) of the Code will take care of the situation. This provision permits the corporation a deduction, and yet the $5,000 comes to the recipient tax-free. To try to go beyond the $5,000 would bring about substantial tax problems, and certainly in planning for the compensation of the shareholder-employee it would not be wise to look forward to relying on this type of payment beyond the $5,000 limit.

F. How About Existing Partnership Agreements for Retired Partners?

Quite often when a professional partnership proceeds to incorporate, there will be a retirement plan which the partnership has had in effect for many years. Some partners may have already retired, relying on the benefits of the retirement plan, and others may be looking forward to retirement shortly, upon the basis of the partnership retirement plan.

Under a partnership retirement plan, it is possible to set up the plan so that the retired partner can receive the retirement benefits while he is in a lower bracket. The portion of the partnership income paid to him will not, of course, be taxed to the other partners who are still active in the firm's business. It will be necessary to convert the form of the partnership retirement plan substantially once a professional corporation is organized. A deferred compensation agreement can be provided as one facet of the solution. The benefits under the corporate pension or profit-sharing plan, as well as fringe benefits, can take up the rest of the slack. Care will need to be taken in setting up compensation for the shareholder-employees of the corporation. Attention will also need to be given as to how goodwill is handled. The existence of a partnership retirement plan need not deter the partners from changing to a corporation.

In the case of the partnership retirement plan, there is no opportunity to set up a trust which can hold investments and which will build up tax-free over a period of years. This is an advantage that the corporate organization affords which cannot be obtained where the enterprise operates in partnership form. Careful evaluation will need to be given, however, to all of the factors involved whenever a partnership which already has a retirement plan in effect converts the partnership into a corporation and then proceeds to adopt a corporate form of retirement plan.

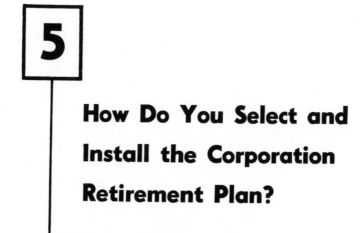

How Do You Select and
Install the Corporation
Retirement Plan?

Certainly one of the principal purposes of incorporation of a professional practice is to establish a corporate entity so that the shareholder-employees may obtain for all of the employees of the corporation, including themselves, the benefits of a pension or profit-sharing plan, or both. This involves two principal aspects, first, the selection of the plan or plans, and second, the installation and qualification of the plans with the Internal Revenue Service. In making the decision as to the type of plan and securing the qualification of it with the Service, competent professional help will be required. All the members of the team, including the attorney, accountant, trust officer, life underwriter, actuary and broker, will generally be needed to bring this about in the best way.

A. Should the Plan Be a Pension or a Profit-Sharing Plan?

The term "retirement" plan includes, basically, two types of plans, the pension plan and the profit-sharing plan. While it might be said that there are also two other types of plans—namely, the annuity plan and the stock bonus plan—the annuity plan is essentially a pension plan and the stock bonus plan is essentially a profit-sharing plan. Consequently, the problem may be resolved into terms of a selection between a pension plan, in its broadest terms, and a profit-sharing plan, or a combination of both.

In order to make a proper decision for the particular situation, it becomes necessary to determine just what a pension plan is and what it does, and similarly, what a profit plan is and what it does.

1. What Is a Pension Plan and What Does It Do?

A pension plan is basically a plan to provide for retirement benefits. It is a plan which is established and maintained by an employer primarily to provide systematically for the payment of definitely determinable benefits to employees over a period of years, usually for life, after their retirement. The retirement benefits are generally measured by and are based upon compensation and years of service of the employees. The determination of the retirement benefits, and the contributions to be made by the employer to the pension plan to provide the benefits, are in no way dependent upon profits. Since the benefits must be definitely determinable, they cannot be increased by funds which may arise from forfeitures of other employees whose services may be terminated for any reason. The test of whether the plan contains definitely determinable benefits depends upon whether the contributions of the employer to the plan can be determined actuarially. In the case of what is called a money purchase pension plan, however, the contributions may be fixed without being geared to profits. A pension plan may provide for the payment of a pension in case of disability and it may also provide for the payment of death benefits through insurance, or otherwise, if such death benefits are "incidental."

The incidental benefits in the form of life insurance may not, in the case of a pension plan, exceed 100 times the anticipated monthly retirement benefits of the employee.

The plan will not be a pension plan if it provides for the payment of other benefits which are not customarily included in a pension plan. Such other benefits would include layoff benefits, or benefits for sickness, accident, hospitalization or medical expenses. The plan must be in writing.

2. What Is a Profit-Sharing Plan and What Does It Do?

A profit-sharing plan is also a written plan which is established and maintained by an employer to provide for the participation in his profits by his employees or their beneficiaries. The plan requires a definite pre-determined formula for allocating the contributions made to the plan among the participants. The formula must also provide for distribution of the funds accumulated under the plan, either after a fixed number of years, the attainment of a stated age of the employee, or upon the prior occurrence of some event such as the employee's layoff, illness, disability, retirement, death or severance from employment. A formula for allocating the contributions among the employees will be definite if, for example, it provides for an allocation of contributions in proportion to their basic compensation. The plan will not qualify, however, even if it contains a definite predetermined formula, if the contributions to the plan are made at such times, or in such amounts, as to make the operation of the plan discriminate in favor of officers, shareholders, highly compensated or supervisory employees. While a profit-sharing plan is primarily a plan of deferred compensation, the amount allocated to the account of an employee may be used to provide incidental life, accident or health insurance for him and his family.

A stock bonus plan is a plan established and maintained by an employer to provide benefits similar to those of a profit-sharing plan. In a stock bonus plan, however, the contributions of the employer are not necessarily dependent upon profits, and the benefits are distributable in stock of the employer. Such a plan is, however, subject to the same requirements as a profit-sharing plan as to allocation and distribution of the stock among the employees or their beneficiaries. A profit-sharing plan is essentially a plan of deferred compensation. If it were to provide for current distributions of profits, or if it were to provide that all compensation should be deferred, it would not be a qualified profit-sharing plan. While the plan does not require a specific contribution formula, since contributions may be left to the discretion of a board of directors, nevertheless there must be a definite allocation formula. This formula may be based on compensation or on compensation and years of service.

While a profit-sharing plan may provide for incidental benefits in the form of life insurance, the premiums paid on ordinary life insurance must not exceed 50% of the contributions allocated to the employee at any time. In such event, the plan must require the trustee of the plan to convert the life insurance contract, at or before retirement, into cash, or provide for periodic income, so that no part of the value of the life insurance policy may be used to continue life insurance protection beyond retirement. As an alternative, the trustee may distribute the life insurance policy to the employee. The cost of the insurance protection is taxable to the employee as paid. In addition, the profit-sharing plan may provide for accident and health insurance for the employee, but the premiums must not exceed 25% of the funds allocated to his account. If both ordinary life insurance and accident and health insurance are provided under the profit-sharing plan, then the amount paid for accident and health insurance, plus one-half of the premiums on the ordinary life insurance, may not exceed 25% of the amount allocated to the account of the employee.

In the case of a profit-sharing plan, forfeitures may be used to increase the interests of the other employees in the plan, generally on the basis of the contributions to the plan for the employees, but in no event may forfeitures be allocated in such fashion as to discriminate in favor of officers, shareholders, supervisory or highly compensated employees.

B. What Kind of Pension Plan?

1. Fixed Benefit Plan

Under a fixed benefit plan, the employee receives, at the time of his retirement, a fixed percentage of his compensation. This may be determined on the basis of an average of the three highest years of the last five years of his employment, or any such readily determinable formula, or combination of years. The percentage may be applied directly to compensation without including any consideration for years of service.

2. Unit Benefit Plan

Under the unit benefit plan a percentage of specified compensation, as in the fixed benefit type of plan, or a fixed sum, is given for each year of service to the corporation. The plan might provide, for example, 1% for each of the first five years of service, 1.5% for the next five years of service and 2% for each year after the first ten, with the total percentage multiplied by the average compensation for three of the five consecutive highest years. Another form of the unit benefit plan would be to provide a specific monthly benefit multiplied by the number of years of service.

3. Flat Benefit Plan

Under the flat benefit plan, the benefit would be a fixed amount per month, as, for example, $100 per month.

4. Money Purchase Plan

Under the money purchase plan, which is really a combination pension and profit-sharing plan, a fixed percentage of compensation, for example 10% of compensation, is contributed by the employer each year and the pension is whatever amount has been accumulated in the account of the particular employee. The commitment by the employer to the plan is without regard to whether there are profits for the year from which to pay. While the amount of the pension cannot be definitely determined, nevertheless the money purchase pension plan is subject to the rules governing pension plans.

5. Variable Annuity Plan

Under the variable annuity plan, benefits are determined by allocating units of the contribution made to the plan, instead of dollars. When the employee retires, his units under the plan will be his portion of the value of all the units under the plan.

6. Annuity Plan

A pension plan may be established with an annuity or insurance contract which sets up a pension plan without the necessity for setting up a trust, since the benefits are paid by the insurance company from whom the annuity is purchased.

C.   What Kind of a Profit-Sharing Plan?

Selection of a profit-sharing plan may involve a choice of several different types of plans, depending upon whether the employer is committed to a fixed percentage of profits or not, and also whether voluntary contributions to the plan will be made by the employees.

How Do You Select and Install the Corporation Retirement Plan?

1. Fixed Percentage Profit-Sharing Plan

A common type of profit-sharing plan will involve the commitment by the employer to pay a fixed percentage of the corporation's profits annually to the plan; for example, 10% of the corporate profits for each year, or a sliding scale, whereby 10% of profits up to $100,000 per year might be committed and 15% of all profits above that amount. The main problem with a fixed percentage formula is that it does not give the Board of Directors any latitude to take into account special factors which arise in a particular year. On the other hand, from the employee's standpoint, it assures him that, if there are corporate profits in any year, then the particular fixed percentage will be contributed to the profit-sharing plan by the employer.

2. Discretionary Formula Plan

A more flexible type of profit-sharing plan will leave to the discretion of the Board of Directors the amount to be contributed to the profit-sharing plan for each year. This gives the Board of Directors the opportunity to decide toward the end of the year whether the condition of the corporation permits the payment of a contribution to the profit-sharing plan, and in what amount. From the standpoint of the employees, such a plan does not, of course, give them as much certainty with respect to their profit-sharing contribution as does a fixed percentage plan.

3. Combined Fixed and Discretionary Percentage Plan

The corporation may set up a profit-sharing plan which is a combined fixed and discretionary percentage plan, with a fixed percentage of profits up to a certain percentage, or up to a particular amount, with discretion of the Board of Directors to make an additional contribution from profits. This type of plan provides, in a sense, the best of both worlds, since it gives the employees a definite fixed commitment of contributions to their profit-sharing account and yet gives the corporation latitude with respect to additional contributions if the profits and other circumstances during a particular year warrant an additional contribution to the plan.

4. Thrift or Savings Plan

The thrift or savings plan is one which generally provides an opportunity to employees to contribute to the plan from their own income anything up to 6% of their yearly salary. The employer then will match the employee's contribution in an amount that is at least equal to 10% of the employee's contribution, and may be as much as 100%. In fact, it may even go up to the 15% of payroll permitted for contributions to profit-sharing plans under the Internal Revenue Code.

D. What Factors Govern the Choice of Plans?

Perhaps the most important decision confronting the shareholders and the Board of Directors of the professional corporation will be the choice of the retirement plan, whether it will be a pension or a profit-sharing plan, or both, and just what type of plan will it be. In making this decision, it will be desirable and necessary to take into account a considerable number of factors to reach the right decision. All of these factors will have to be carefully considered and evaluated. Among the most important of these factors are the contributions, benefits and costs.

1. Contributions

Under a pension plan, the contributions to the plan are a fixed commitment; whereas, under a profit-sharing plan the contributions may be quite flexible, depending upon whether a fixed percentage of the profits is required to be made to the plan. In any event, the contribution to a profit-sharing plan will vary with the corporate profits each year.

Under a pension plan, the contribution required will be determined by what it takes, actuarially, to provide the funds necessary to make the payment of the pension when the employee reaches retirement age. Where the pension plan is funded with life insurance, the contribution, in the form of premium payments, will, of course, need to be made regularly and the same is true where the pension is funded with an annuity. Where, however, the pension is funded with other types of investment under a trusteed plan, the payments to the trust may be more flexible, since the amounts actuarially required may be overpaid in good years and underpaid in lean years, although the least that can be paid in the lean years will be the interest required on the fund needed to provide the pension at the time of the employee's retirement. In a trusteed plan, for practical purposes, if the maximum overpayment is made for two successive years, it will generally be possible to skip payments altogether in the third year. Similarly, if the maximum overpayment is made for a number of years, then it will be possible to skip payments altogether for about half that number of years.

Contributions to a pension plan are not limited to any fixed percentage of payroll of the corporation, but may be made in whatever amount is actuarially determined to be necessary to fund the pension plan; in other words, to provide the funds needed to pay the pensions due the employees as they reach retirement age. In the case of a profit-sharing plan, however, the Internal Revenue Code limits the contributions to the plan to a maximum of 15% of payroll for all participants in the plan.

2. Benefits

In the case of a pension plan, the benefits payable to the employees may not be reduced by the employer unless required by business necessity. The mere fact that the corporation has lost money that year will not of itself constitute such a business necessity for a pension plan. In the case of a profit-sharing plan, however, since the contribution to the plan is geared to profits, there will not be any amounts at all allocated to the accounts of the employees where the corporation experiences losses, rather than profits in a particular year.

3. Costs

The costs of a pension plan are fixed and determinable in advance; whereas, those of a profit-sharing plan are flexible and will vary according to the profits of the corporation and the degree of fixed commitment under the profit-sharing plan.

In the case of a pension plan, forfeitures resulting from the fact that some employees leave the employ of the corporation can be used only to reduce the payments of the corporation to the plan. They cannot be allocated among the remaining participants in the plan. In the case of a profit-sharing plan, however, forfeitures may be allocated among the remaining participants or be used to apply to the employer's costs. Any allocation of forfeitures among the participants must, however, be made in such fashion as not to discriminate in favor of shareholders, officers, supervisory or highly compensated employees.

4. Vesting

In a pension plan, there may be provision that the interest of an employee vests after a specified number of years, or the plan may provide that the interest does not vest until the employee reaches retirement age, or is permanently disabled, or dies. In the case of a profit-sharing plan, the interest of the employee must vest within a specified period of years and, generally speaking, the vesting period may be spread over a period of years, but that period of years may not generally exceed ten to 15 years at the most.

5. Integration of the Plan

The effect of "integrating" a plan is to enable the employer to take into account, in setting up a pension or profit-sharing plan, the fact that Social Security already provides substantial benefits to all employees with respect to that portion of their earnings on which Social Security taxes are payable. The integration rules merely permit the employer to take that fact into account in designing the pension or profit-sharing plan which is to be integrated with Social Security.

The rules with respect to integration of the plan are different as between pension and profit-sharing plans. Social Security provides a pension of about 37½% on a $9,000 income. In the case of pension plans, integration with Social Security is subject to a rule that the pension plan may provide retirement benefits equal to 37½% of average annual compensation above $9,000. If the plan includes disability benefits, the rate drops to 33.75%. In order to provide higher benefits than that, the plan will have to provide a corresponding benefit to employees whose compensation is less than $9,000.

In the case of profit-sharing plans, the plan may be integrated with Social Security; that is, allocating employer contributions on the basis of compensation above $9,000 per year. The maximum percentage differential that can exist, however, between contributions on compensation above $9,000 and that below such figure, is 7% of pay.

If the employer has adopted both a pension and a profit-sharing plan, then only one of the plans may be fully integrated.

E. How Do You Select Your Particular Retirement Plan?

With all of the factors and options open to an employer in selecting a retirement plan, the question arises as to which particular combination of plans will be best for the particular employer. The answer depends upon all of the facts and circumstances. For the older professional, who is looking forward to the possibility of retiring in a few years, or if not retiring, at least to the possibility that he might be able to retire if he decided to do so, the pension plan, particularly a money purchase plan or a fixed benefit plan, which would assure him of a retirement income which is a substantial portion of his present compensation, would seem to be best.

For the young professional, who has just started out in his profession, and who has many other obligations which involve raising a family, paying for a mortgage on his house and catching up on many things that he and his wife have wished they could afford, the prospect of making substantial payments to provide a fixed benefit or money purchase pension for his fellow shareholder-employees, would not seem too attractive. From his standpoint, the profit-sharing plan, with the opportunity to build up a substantial fund over a considerable period of years, would seem better. In most cases, a combination of both a pension plan and a profit-sharing plan, or for that matter, a thrift or savings plan, would seem advisable to consider, if not adopt.

The choice between insurance and stocks as an investment for the plan introduces another factor of importance. Each type of investment has its own built-in proponents. The mutual fund salesman will naturally have arguments in favor of his product and the life underwriter will have his preference.

The simplicity of the plan will need to be considered. The profit-sharing plan, not requiring the services of an actuary, will seem simpler and easier to adopt. If the shareholders of the professional corporation talk in terms of an insured pension plan, the insurance company will make it clear that they can provide the actuarial services to the corporation free of any actuarial cost. On the other hand, the actuarial firm will be able to point out that if the pension plan is not an insured plan, then there will be greater flexibility with respect to the contributions to the plan, since there will not be the annual recurring cost of insurance premiums, and that contributions may be overpaid in two years, with the opportunity to skip contributions altogether in the third year if that is done. The proponents of profit-sharing plans will point out that, as to contributions, certainly, profit-sharing plans are far more flexible than pension plans. The proponent of the pension plan will observe that pension plans do not have to vest in a few years, as do profit-sharing plans, so that the employees are less likely to leave the corporate employment if they are covered by a pension plan. Those who espouse life insurance for pension and profit-sharing plans will also point out that by investing the funds in a life insurance policy, or an annuity, the need for the trustee services will be that much less. In talking to the trustee, however, he will quickly point out that administrative costs are included in setting the insurance premiums involved in the purchase of the life insurance. For those who are injudicious enough to consider acting as their own trustees, there is the temptation of shortcutting on the trustees' fees altogether and indulging in the rather expensive privilege of handling their own investments, as well as handling the administration of the trust fund. All in all, it would be well to consider that handling a pension or profit-sharing trust is a job for professionals and in this respect, as in most others, as Lincoln observed, "The laborer is worthy of his hire."

It would seem well for the shareholders of the professional corporation to make sure that in considering all of these matters, they have informed, professional and objective advice, insofar as possible. Certainly this is an area that requires careful and deliberate consideration, to make sure that no stone is unturned and that the decisions which are made are not arrived at on the basis of shallow or shortsighted decisions.

F. How About Master or Prototype Plans?

In recent years, the use of master or prototype plans has been encouraged by the Internal Revenue Service in order to facilitate the consideration of retirement plans, since one determination letter may serve to cover a multitude of individual employers, all of whom adopt the master or prototype plans. The use of such master or prototype plans may prove desirable in some cases.

How Do You Select and Install the Corporation Retirement Plan?

1. What Are the Advantages of Such Plans?

The development of the master and prototype pension plan was a natural step from the adoption of the Keogh or H.R. 10 Plan. The Keogh Plan is, basically, a uniform type plan, with the specifications designated by Congress and the Internal Revenue Service in the statutory and regulatory restrictions which are imposed upon all Keogh-type plans. These restrictions afforded benefits to the employer, in terms of reduced costs and simplicity of the plan, and, at the same time, afforded benefits to the Internal Revenue Service in terms of simplification of its handling of each plan. The difference between master and prototype plans is that, in the master plan, the funding organization is specified; whereas, in a prototype plan the funding organization will be specified by the particular employer in adopting the plan. In virtually all other respects, they are similar. The purpose, of course, is to eliminate the need for each employer to have its own plan specially designed and qualified.

Not only is the master and prototype plan attractive to the employer and the Internal Revenue Service because of its simplicity and uniformity, it is attractive to the life insurance and mutual fund industries, because it is attractively packaged and can be sold as a "product," requiring no drafting or adaptation. Consequently, it can be delivered by the salesman to the employer, without requiring the additional services of a lawyer, accountant or actuary. The life insurance industry was mainly instrumental in urging upon the Internal Revenue Service the adoption of master and prototype plans. In this effort, it naturally had the good wishes of the banking and mutual fund industry as well, since they, as well as brokerage houses, could market this type of plan to advantage.

Naturally, the small employer, because of the attraction of reduced costs and simplicity of adoption and administration of the plan, would be receptive to a sales presentation of the master and prototype plan. The larger employer, more conscious of the restrictions and shortcomings of a uniform and restricted plan, and more able to bear the costs of a tailor-made plan, would be less receptive to the sales presentation made on behalf of master and prototype plans. Most professional corporations, other than those with only very few shareholders, will generally wish to have a tailor-made plan which fits the particular needs and purposes of the respective corporation and its shareholders. The savings in legal, accounting and

126

actuarial fees effected by the adoption of a master or prototype plan may be more than offset by the loss of flexibility in design of the plan to fit the particular needs of the corporation and its shareholders.

2. Should It Be a Standardized or a Variable Plan?

Master and prototype plans may be of a "standardized" form, in which case they have virtually no options open for the particular employer, or "variable," in which case the particular employer has his choice of many different options. These options pertain to such aspects as coverage, vesting, contributions, benefits and choice of investments, in addition to the basic choice as between a pension or profit-sharing plan. Use of the standardized plan, while it may save money at the outset, will subject the parties to rigid restrictions that may, in the long run, prove difficult to live with, even for the one-man corporation.

To make the point, selecting a plan may be compared to buying a suit of clothes. The standardized plan merely gives one the right size of suit. The variable plan not only gives the right size, it also gives a choice as to whether the suit should be a long, short or regular. The tailor-made plan is the same as a tailor-made suit. It should provide a perfect fit for the customer or client.

3. What Problems Are Involved?

The situation with master and prototype plans is one where the pressures on all concerned may tend to encourage the employer to turn primarily to a salesman for professional advice. This may not only be stimulated by the zeal and industry of the salesman himself, but is often encouraged by the determination of the employer to save on the costs of the plan and the desire to find a simple solution. Unfortunately, however, the salesman may not always temper his zeal with caution and sometimes may not be too concerned with his inability to be entirely objective on the employer's behalf. Certainly there is no reason to lay the blame entirely on the salesman for taking on the role of advisor to the employer, particularly if the employer, with or without the advice of his lawyer and accountant, encourages the salesman to do so. Part of the problem may lie in the fact that the lawyer and accountant, who should be advising the employer, either fail to provide him with the measure of advice and counsel that the employer needs, or they may not be brought into the picture at all by the employer, due to his failure to understand or his desire to cut costs. Certainly the employer's lawyer and accountant, when he is looking to them for advice in these matters, should not, through neglect or bad advice, prevent the employer from obtaining the benefits of a proper pension or profit-sharing plan. The salesman who presents the plan to the employer certainly has the right to pursue his selling, provided he does not venture too far afield in his role of advisor, in addition to that of salesman. The employer, on the other hand, needs to bear in mind that if he takes his advice from the salesman alone, he may be obtaining it from one whose main object is to sell, and from one who may or may not be adequately informed, impartial and objective, subject to professional discipline and farsighted.

Master plans may tend to exclude the advice of the lawyer and accountant on the various options that are available to the employer. These options involve five major areas of decision. The most important of the decisions on which legal advice will be needed is that relating to the choice of plan; that is, whether it is to be a pension or profit-sharing plan. In addition, the advice of counsel should be obtained on the question of who are to be eligible for coverage, what are to be the contributions to the plan and what will be the terms of vesting and benefits. In addition, counsel will be needed on the question of discrimination in favor of the officer, shareholder, highly paid and supervisory employees and on prohibited transactions. These latter items will involve continued counsel, not merely at the outset of the plan, but also during its operation. Violations in these respects can disqualify the plan. To the extent that adoption of a master plan might lead the employer to overlook the necessity for competent professional advice on these matters, the decision could, in the long run, prove shortsighted and costly.

G. How Do You Install the Plan?

Once the decision has been made to adopt a retirement plan, or a combination of plans, the next question is as to the requirements which must be met with respect to installation of the plan. How is that done? The plan, in order to qualify for the beneficial tax treatment provided by the Internal Revenue Code, both as to the corporation and employees, as well as making the trust itself tax-exempt, must be shown to meet certain

How Do You Select and Install the Corporation Retirement Plan?

basic requirements set forth in the Internal Revenue Code. When this is done, the plan will, after the submission of all the necessary data to the Internal Revenue Service, then be held qualified, through the issuance of a determination letter by the Service.

1. What Are the Basic Requirements?

A retirement plan, whether it be a pension plan, profit-sharing plan or stock bonus plan, must have certain attributes which are required of every qualified plan. The plan must be in writing. It must be communicated to the employees. The trust which forms a part of the plan must, in order to be a qualified and exempt trust under the Internal Revenue Code, be created or organized in the United States and maintained as a domestic trust. It must be part of a plan established by the employer for the exclusive benefit of his employees or their beneficiaries. Its purpose must be the distribution to the employees or their beneficiaries of the corpus and income of the trust fund in accordance with the plan. Moreover, it must be impossible, under the trust instrument, at any time prior to the satisfaction of all liabilities to the employees and their beneficiaries under the trust, for any part of the trust corpus or income to be used for, or diverted to, any purpose other than the exclusive benefit of the employees or their beneficiaries.

The plan must be a permanent, as distinguished from a temporary, program. While the employer may reserve the right to change or terminate the plan and to discontinue contributions, the abandonment of the plan for any reason other than business necessity within a few years after it has been put into effect will be evidence that the plan, from its inception, was not a bona fide program for the exclusive benefit of the employees in general. While a profit-sharing plan does not require contributions by the employer each year, or even that it contribute the same amount, or in accordance with the same ratio every year; nevertheless, a single or occasional contribution out of profits for employees does not establish a bona fide profit-sharing plan. In order to have such a plan, there must be recurring and substantial contributions out of profits for the employees. If the plan is abandoned, the employer must notify the District Director promptly. The plan may not be designed as a subterfuge for the distribution of profits to shareholders. It need not, however, provide benefits for all employees in general, although it may not discriminate in favor of of-

129

ficers or shareholder-employees, or those who are highly compensated or supervisory employees.

2. Who Must Be Included in the Plan?

The Internal Revenue Code sets forth specific rules as to who must be covered by a plan in order for it to qualify. The plan must include 70% or more of all the employees or 80% or more of all those who are eligible to benefit if 70% or more of all the employees are eligible to benefit. There may be excluded from these employees any who have not been employed for five years, or whose employment is temporary; that is, less than 20 hours per week, or less than five months in any calendar year. In addition, the Code permits other classifications, such as confining the plan to salaried employees alone, if the classification is determined by the Service not to be discriminatory in favor of officers, shareholders or highly compensated or supervisory employees.

3. How Is the Plan Qualified?

In order to obtain a determination letter from the Service to the effect that the plan is qualified, information with respect to the plan must be submitted with the request for the determination letter, including specific information with respect to the 25 highest paid employees covered by the plan. While an advance determination letter from the Service is not required; nevertheless, obtaining such a determination letter will permit amendment of the plan to eliminate the possibility of disqualification and the consequent loss of deductions for contributions to the plan. The plan should contain provisions for its proper amendment and termination. As an alternative to termination, a plan may be suspended, although suspension may, in time, develop into a discontinuance. This, in turn, becomes a termination of the plan, without having complied with the formal steps generally involved in termination.

H. How May a Plan Become Disqualified?

In considering the plan, whether it be a pension plan or a profit-sharing plan, the problem of later disqualification of the plan, even though the plan was properly qualified at the time it was instituted, becomes a matter of considerable importance. The principal ground for disqualification of a plan, even though it was properly qualified at the time it was set up, generally results from discrimination in its operation or from engagement in prohibited transactions.

1. How May a Plan Be Disqualified for Discrimination?

In two recent Circuit Court decisions, profit-sharing plans were held to be unqualified because of discrimination resulting from a formula giving weight to years of service.[1] In one case, the profit-sharing plan of a medical clinic weighted service, experience and education under a point system which discriminated in favor of the doctors, and particularly one of them. In the other case, years of service, including pre-plan years, gave the only shareholder a percentage three to five points higher than most of the other employees.

In a recent Tax Court case a Subchapter S tax-option corporation, which had adopted a pension plan for its salaried employees, but not for its other employees, was held to have discriminated in its plan, despite the fact that the non-salaried employees were unionized and could have bargained for coverage under the plan, but the union decided not to.[2]

A corporate plan which gives a retirement benefit of 50% of career average compensation has been held to qualify even though an officer-shareholder, who receives 80% of the current compensation paid by the employer, will be expected to receive a substantial portion of the total pension benefits under the plan. The benefits bear a uniform relationship to compensation.[3]

2. When Will a Qualification of a Plan Be Revoked Retroactively?

Suppose that a plan has been qualified and has been operated for a number of years. Employees have come and gone. Forfeitures have occurred. The number of non-shareholder employees has diminished greatly, but the number of shareholder-employees has increased. Suppose also that the forfeitures of the non-shareholder employees will, it appears, cause the benefits under the plan of the shareholder-employees to increase. Can

---

[1] Auner v. United States, 440 F.2d 516 (C. A. 7, 1971); McMenamy v. United States, 442 F.2d 359 (C. A. 8, 1971).
[2] Loevsky v. Comm'r, 55 T.C.–No. 106 (1971).
[3] Rev. Rul. 71-255, IRB 1971-24, 34.

the Service rule that the plan, which once was qualified, no longer is a qualified plan?

The Service has held [4] that except in rare or unusual circumstances, the revocation or modification of a ruling will not be applied retroactively if: (1) there has been no misstatement or omission of material facts; (2) the facts subsequently developed are not materially different from the facts on which the ruling was based; (3) there has been no change in the applicable law; (4) the ruling was originally issued with respect to a prospective or proposed transaction; (5) the taxpayer acted in good faith in reliance upon the ruling, and the retroactive revocation would be to his detriment.

In actual practice, it appears that the Service may retroactively revoke a favorable ruling on a plan if it appears that under the plan the allocation of forfeitures to the participants in the plan is made on the basis of account balances and such allocation would, on the facts, operate in a discriminatory fashion against the non-shareholder employees. Accordingly, it is necessary to check a plan each year to make sure that the facts and circumstances have not changed to such a degree that a plan, which was not discriminatory when adopted, has now become discriminatory because of a change in facts as the years have passed by. The Service has recently ruled that a profit-sharing plan will not fail to qualify merely because it allocates forfeitures on the basis of account balances.[5]

3. What Are Prohibited Transactions?

A pension or profit-sharing plan is a plan for the benefit of the employees. If it is used in such fashion as to not be for the exclusive benefit of the employees, then the transactions involved may constitute prohibited transactions and result in disqualification of the plan. An example of this would be the lending of money or other property from the plan to the corporation itself, or to one or more of the shareholders, without adequate and proper collateral. The management of a corporation which considers that its pension or profit-sharing plan is just another corporate asset, to be used for the benefit of the corporation or for its shareholders, can quickly cause disqualification of the plan. One way to avoid such prohibited trans-

---

4 Rev. Proc. 69-1, 1969-CB, 381, 386.
5 Rev. Rul. 71-4, 1971-1 IRB 15.

actions is to make sure that the trustee of the plan is an independent outside entity, such as the trust department of a bank. Such an outside trustee is more likely to prevent self-dealing by the officers and directors of the corporation and to make sure that loans to the corporation or to the shareholders are made at arm's length and with proper and adequate collateral.

4. Are There Special Standards for Professional Corporations?

An interesting development has been taking place in some of the field offices of the Internal Revenue Service. Special requirements as to vesting are being imposed upon profit-sharing plans of all small corporations. For example, in Texas the Service holds: (1) where there are less than three non-shareholder employees, there must be 100% vesting after one year; (2) where there are from three to ten, there must be vesting of 20% per year, with 100% vesting at the end of five years; (3) where there are ten or more, there must be 100% vesting in ten years, with a waiting period of three years allowed. When there are ten or less shareholder-employees, eligibility age for qualification under the plan must not be more than 21 years. Less stringent vesting rules apply to pension plans.

Whether special rules for each field office will be permitted or whether an overall national policy on these special rules will be worked out still remains to be seen. At present, it appears that each field office is free to impose such of the Keogh Plan limitations as it desires to prevent what that field office feels might lead to discrimination. It appears there will need to be closer coordination on these special rules, as there certainly need to be uniform rules on a national basis.

I. What Happens to the Keogh Fund if You Incorporate?

In many cases, a group of professionals who wish to consider incorporation, in order to obtain the additional benefits that come with incorporation, will have an existing Keogh Plan. What can they do with the funds that are already in the Keogh Plan? Can they transfer those to the corporate plan?

The Regulations have for some time made it clear that the Keogh Plan limitation of $2,500 or 10% of earned income does not apply to the contributions to a corporate pension or profit-sharing plan on a person's behalf under such plan, even though he is participating already in an H.R.

10 plan. He cannot, however, in such a situation, participate in the H.R. 10 plan as a self-employed person, although he can participate in the corporate plan as a self-employed individual.[6]

A group which has a Keogh Plan can, of course, when it changes over to a corporate plan, continue the Keogh Plan, for the benefit of those covered under the Keogh Plan, by "freezing" the assets of the Keogh Plan for the benefit of those who were covered by the plan at the time the corporate plan was adopted. The Service has, in an unpublished ruling,[7] indicated that the assets of a Keogh Plan can be transferred to the corporate plan, as a published ruling[8] permits transfers between qualified corporate trusts. The assets must be transferred from one trustee to the other and cannot be made available to the employees themselves. The benefits cannot, however, be paid to owner-employees except in accordance with the Keogh Plan rules and regulations. In addition, it is essential that the Service be notified of the transfer.[9] An alternative which could also be adopted would be to terminate the Keogh Plan, but in the case of owner-employees who have not reached the age of 59½ years, this would constitute a premature distribution, with a penalty tax imposed for the premature distribution, unless the distribution is taken in the form of a non-transferable deferred annuity, paying no benefits prior to age 59½, or in the form of a United States government retirement bond.[10]

In each situation, the various alternatives will need to be carefully considered if there is already an existing Keogh Plan. Generally, it would seem best to transfer the Keogh assets to the corporate plan, but with extreme care, to make sure that all of the rules with respect to such assets are complied with in every detail. Where the shareholder-employees themselves are trustees of the corporate plan there can be grave danger that, in administering the corporate plan, they may overlook the fact that the Keogh Plan assets are subject to Keogh Plan rules, rather than to the corporate plan rules. For this reason a corporate trustee will, in such cases, be a very necessary safeguard against possible violation of the Keogh Plan rules by the trustees. In addition, by requesting a ruling from the Service

---

6 Reg. 1.404(e)-1(d).
7 Special Ruling, Feb. 18, 1971.
8 Rev. Rul. 67-213, 1967-2, C.B. 149.
9 See Rev. Rul. 69-252, 1969-1 C.B. 128.
10 Reg. 1.402(a)-1(a)(2); Reg. 1.405-3.

at the time of the transfer,[11] the transaction can be protected from later attack.

J. How About Voluntary Contributions to a Plan?

In many cases a professional group which is considering the adoption of a pension or profit-sharing plan may wish to consider the possibility of making voluntary contributions to the plan in years when they have extra money to contribute. To protect the shareholder-employees with respect to their right to make voluntary contributions, it will be important to provide in the plan for such contributions. This generally will not be feasible in the case of insurance as an investment of the plan, since it would require the purchase of smaller individual policies. The voluntary contributions, when made, should be separately accounted for and should be, as a rule, invested in securities. Provision for withdrawal of the voluntary contributions, as well as the profit accumulated thereon, should be retained for the employees. While the contribution will not give rise to a tax deduction, it will permit the employees to set aside amounts which can accumulate, tax-free, over the years, and still be accessible to them. Voluntary contributions cannot exceed 10% of the employee's total compensation while he is covered by the plan, but if there is provision in the plan for voluntary contributions, the contributions can be made in a later year and take advantage of the possibility of contributing up to 10% of the employee's total contribution for the period he has been under the plan.[12] If a professional corporation adopts a master or prototype plan, it will be most important to determine that the plan permits voluntary contributions, as well as withdrawal of the contributions and of the profits thereon. By providing for voluntary contributions under a profit-sharing plan, a means will be made available to the employees to engage in voluntary saving programs, with the funds readily accessible, perhaps upon 60 days' notice. It will provide the employees with a method for setting aside funds for unusual emergencies or investment possibilities, while at the same time assuring themselves of tax-free accumulations on those funds as long as they are under the plan. Through the voluntary contributions the shareholder-

---

[11] Rev. Proc. 69-1 C.B. 381.
[12] Rev. Rul. 59-185, 1959-1 C.B. 86; Rev. Rul. 69-217, 1969-1 C.B. 115.

employee can retain a great deal of flexibility over his investment, and yet, through the tax-free accumulation, he can build up, over a period of years, a very substantial amount of investment that is as readily available to him as would be money generally invested in securities or in savings accounts. When coupled with his basic profit-sharing plan, whether coupled also with a pension plan, he can have, in a sense, the best of both worlds.

K. What Can Be Done for the Senior Professional?

In the case of many professional groups, one or more of the professionals may be at an age where the cost of a fixed benefit pension plan might appear to be too high, particularly where the cost to the other shareholder-employees is concerned, and yet a profit-sharing plan would not accomplish a substantial benefit to the senior professional because there are not enough years left in which to accumulate profits for his benefit. In such a case, a money purchase pension plan might prove to be the answer. Let us assume a situation involving a doctor who is 60 years of age. He may have five or ten productive years left in which to accumulate profits under a profit-sharing plan, but in his case this might not do as much for him as he would like. By setting up a money purchase pension plan, it will be possible to provide an answer for him. In his case, a 60% money purchase accumulation, at 5% per annum, to normal retirement age 65, with a life expectancy of 15 years, will provide him with an annual pension equal to approximately 22% of his compensation. Such a plan would, on those facts, probably prove acceptable to the Service.[13]

In the case of a 40-year-old man, however, a 60% money purchase plan would, at 5% per annum, result in a pension of about 190% of his compensation at age 65. In his case, the plan would run afoul of the general principle under Section 401(a) of the Internal Revenue Code that a pension must be a supplement to an employee's current compensation. It cannot be the "predominant" method of compensation. As a supplement to the employee's current compensation, the pension provides something to the employee over and above his current compensation and the total must

---

[13] Isidore Goodman, Chapter on "Master and Prototype Pension and Profit-Sharing Plans in Operation," *Corporate Master and Prototype Retirement Plans,* Practising Law Institute, 1970.

be reasonable.[14] Where the cost of the pension is a major portion of the employee's compensation, it will be not a supplement but the major portion of his compensation on an overall basis. Accordingly, while a 60% money purchase plan may well be justifiable in the case of a shareholder-employee who is 60 years of age, where there are other shareholder-employees who are 40 years of age or younger, then a contribution to the money purchase pension plan, on an overall basis, may, as a rule of thumb, be unacceptable if it exceeds 25% of the annual compensation.[15] In the case of a one-man corporation, where the only shareholder-employee is over 50 years of age, the money purchase pension plan may prove to be the solution. This might also apply in a situation where there are several shareholder-employees who are over 50 years of age. In each case, it will be necessary, of course, to obtain approval from the Service with respect to the plan and to make sure that as the years pass by, the plan does not become discriminatory because of changes in the covered group. A plan which is approved on one set of facts, may, over a period of years, due to deaths, retirement or dismissal of employees, become discriminatory, because the balance between the shareholder, officer, supervisory and highly paid employees, on the one hand, and the other employees on the other, may cause the plan to discriminate against the latter group.

---

[14] Reg. 1.404(a)-1(b).
[15] See Footnote 13.

6

How Is Insurance Used in the Professional Corporation?

In the case of professional corporations, as in virtually all other fields of combined business and legal questions, insurance plays a very important if not major role. The proper utilization of insurance of many kinds can make the professional corporation more effective, not only for the corporation itself, but for the shareholders and employees as well. Much of the benefits of the professional corporation are and should be effected through the use of insurance.

At the outset, certain types of insurance, such as malpractice and casualty insurance on the various types of property used in the operation of the professional corporation's business, will need to be transferred from the predecessor partnership or proprietorship. It may be that in some instances, the same coverage would be carried over. In others, new policies will be issued. Certainly in planning for the transfer, competent professional advice in the insurance field, from the chartered underwriter, whether it be in the field of property insurance or life insurance, will be advisable. The cost of malpractice insurance should be the same for the corporation as for the predecessor partnership or proprietorship, but in California, for some unexplained reason, malpractice insurance for professional corporations has been somewhat higher in rates than the malpractice insurance of the predecessor partnership or proprietorship. Such higher rates would not, however, appear to be justified in light of the facts, and it appears that in time the rates, except for the upward and apparently constant thrust of inflation, should be the same, regardless of whether the entity in question is a professional corporation or a partnership or proprietorship.

A. How Are Health and Accident, Medical and Disability Insurance Handled?

One of the most important advantages of the professional corporation lies in the fact that the corporation may pay the premiums on health and accident and medical and disability insurance and deduct the premiums. At the same time, the premiums do not constitute taxable income to the employees of the professional corporation. Similarly, disability insurance may be provided by the corporation and a medical reimbursement plan adopted. Payment of the premiums for the disability insurance, as well as payments to the employee, by way of the medical reimbursement, will be deductible by the corporation, without such payments constituting taxable income to the employees of the corporation.

In the case of a partnership or proprietorship, the deductibility of medical expense payments is limited, since they constitute deductions only to the extent that they exceed 3% of the taxpayer's adjusted gross income. Health and accident insurance premiums are deductible without regard to the 3% limitation for one-half of the amount paid for medical care insurance for the taxpayer, his spouse or a dependent. The deduction may not, however, exceed $150 per year. The premium which is deductible is only the premium for medical care insurance. The remaining one-half of the cost of medical care insurance, together with any excess over the $150 limit, is deductible, subject to the 3% limitation.[1]

---

[1] Internal Revenue Code, Sec. 213.

How Is Insurance Used in the Professional Corporation?

1. What Types of Payment May Be Excluded by the Employee from His Gross Income?

(a) *Accident and Health Insurance*

Under Section 105 of the Code, it is provided that amounts received by an employee through accident or health insurance for personal injuries or sickness must be included in gross income to the extent that such amounts are: (1) attributable to contributions by the employer which were not includable in the gross income of the employee; (2) are paid by the employer. Certain exceptions to the general rule, however, permit the employee to exclude many such payments from his gross income. Among such payments which can be excluded from the employee's gross income are the amounts of any payments which are made to reimburse the employee, directly or indirectly, for medical care expenses incurred by him for himself, his spouse and his dependents. Where the employee has himself taken a deduction on his individual income tax return for medical expenses, the amount reimbursed to him by the employer will not be excluded from his taxable income.

(b) *Disability Payments*

Payments may also be excluded from the employee's gross income if they constitute payment for permanent disability of the employee himself, or of his spouse or a dependent. In addition, the employee may exclude payments which constitute wages, or payments in lieu of wages, for absence from work on account of personal injuries or sickness. Such payments may be excluded from the employee's income up to a weekly rate of $75 during the first 30 calendar days of his absence from work if the payments do not exceed 75% of his regular weekly rate of wages. This will not apply to the first seven calendar days, unless the employee is hospitalized for at least one day during such period. After the first 30 days, the payments which may be excluded increase to a weekly rate of $100.

(c) *Payments Under an Accident or Health Plan for Employees*

Where the payments received by the employee are not received through accident or health insurance, the Internal Revenue Code provides that if the payments are received under an "accident or health plan for employees," then they will be treated as amounts received through accident or health insurance.

2. What Constitutes an Accident or Health Plan?

The Treasury Regulations [2] provide that there may be different plans for different employees or classes of employees. A plan may be either insured or non-insured. It need not be in writing, nor need the employee's rights to benefits under the plan be enforceable. Even if the employee's rights are not enforceable, the Regulations provide that an amount will be deemed to be received under the plan if, at the time the employee was injured or became sick, he was covered by a plan, "or a program, policy or custom having the effect of a plan," providing for the payment of amounts to the employee in case of injury or sickness, and if notice or knowledge of the plan was reasonably available to the employee.

(a) *May Such a Plan Discriminate?*

The Code does not require that medical reimbursement plans be non-discriminatory, as it does require in the case of pension and profit-sharing plans. The Code does, however, require that medical reimbursement plans be plans for "employees," in order to obtain the tax benefits provided by the Code for a proper plan.

The Tax Court has held that a plan which covered only two stockholder-employees out of 50 employees was valid, since a plan could discriminate among employees, provided that it was a plan for them as "employees," even though those employees who were covered by the plan were stockholders. [3] There was no written plan and the shareholders were equal in their holdings and were officers.

(b) *How About a Plan for Stockholders?*

In another case, however, where the Court found that the plan was for "stockholders," and not for employees, the plan was held not to comply with the provisions of the Code. [4] In that case, the medical reimbursement payments were made to employees who were, with a single exception, officers, shareholders or members of their families. There was no written evidence of a corporate program, nor was any notice of the plan given to the employees. Discretion as to which of the employees would be covered

---

[2] Treasury Regulations, Sec. 1.105-5(a).
[3] Bogene, Inc., 27 T.C.M. 730 (1968).
[4] Alan B. Larkin, 48 T.C. 629 (1967), affd 394 F.2d 494 (CAl, 1968).

by the plan was left with the officers of the corporation. The Court held that the plan favored the shareholders as a class rather than the employees. Accordingly, it did not meet the provisions of the Code. The existence of a plan, in the opinion of the Court, was doubtful.

In another case,[5] where the Tax Court found that the primary purpose for the incorporation of a business and the adoption of its medical plan was one of tax avoidance, the Court held the plan invalid, since it benefitted the shareholder-employee in his capacity as an owner of the business, rather than as an employee. Consequently, where a plan purports to be for the employees, if those employees are also the shareholders of the corporation, then the Court will certainly give serious thought to whether the plan is in fact a plan for the employees, in accordance with the Code provisions.

(c) Should the Plan Be in Writing?

Since the Code and the Regulations make it clear that a written plan will qualify for the tax benefits, it certainly would be well to have the plan set forth in writing. It should cover all, or certainly as many of the employees as possible. Moreover, the plan should be made known to the employees in advance so that when the employee should become ill or injured, there would be no question of his coverage and the extent thereof.

In a case where the only officers and shareholders of a corporation were covered under a written medical reimbursement program, which was expressly limited to include "only employees who shall be also an officer of the corporation," the Tax Court held that a valid plan existed and, since the shareholder-employees were the key management employees, they constituted a natural category of employees and the plan for their reimbursement complied with the statute.[6] They were the only employees performing management type work.

(d) What if the Plan Does Not Meet the Statutory Tests?

Where the plan in question does not comply with the statute, the payments made by the corporation might still possibly be deducted as compensation to the employees in question. If, however, they are shareholder-employees, and the amounts paid to them under the medical reimbursement

---

[5] Edward D. Smithback, 28 T.C.M. 709 (1969).
[6] E. B. Smith, 29 T.C.M. 1065 (1970).

plan, when added to their other compensation, result in an unreasonable amount of compensation, then the medical reimbursement payments may constitute dividends to them as shareholders.[7]

While it is apparent that the Tax Court has upheld a number of plans which were discriminatory and exclusively for shareholders or officers of a corporation, it would appear imprudent to rely too heavily upon these decisions in planning for an accident or health plan. It would appear safe to say that any plan which tests the bounds of reasonableness is likely to be suspect in the eyes of the Internal Revenue Service. Playing games with the Service is a rather expensive sport. Moreover, adopting a plan which is discriminatory among the employees of a corporation can prove damaging to morale and more costly in the long run than would the adequate provision of reasonably commensurate benefits for all employees across the board. The management of a professional corporation would be improvident indeed to attempt to provide a health and accident plan merely for the stockholder-employees.

B. Life Insurance as an Investment of the Retirement Trust

1. How Do You Handle Investments of the Plan?

The retirement plan may be either an insured or a trusteed plan. If it is a profit-sharing plan or money purchase pension plan, then up to one half of the amounts contributed to the plan by the employer may be invested in life insurance. Under insured fixed-benefit pension plans, the amounts must be "incidental."

In a trusteed plan, the funds may be invested in any monetary enterprise permitted by local law to be made by a trustee in the particular state involved. Generally speaking, since the trust will be an exempt entity for income tax purposes, it will be desirable to invest the funds in enterprises which will yield a high income, while at the same time being a safe investment. Ground rents will generally be a very good investment, since they return a very high yield, as a rule. Tax-shelter type investments (for example, depreciable real estate or equipment), would not ordinarily be a desirable type of investment, since the tax shelter is of no value whatso-

---

[7] Sanders and Sons, Inc., 26 T.C.M. 671 (1967).

ever to the retirement trust, it being a tax-exempt entity. Investment in the stock of the employer corporation itself may prove proper, in some cases, although care must be taken to make sure that such an investment does not constitute a "prohibited" transaction, which would cause the trust to lose its exemption. To determine whether such an investment might or might not be prohibited, it will be advisable to obtain a determination letter from the District Director's office. Loans to the employer corporation or its shareholders will constitute prohibited transactions, unless they are properly and adequately secured. It would be best to avoid them.

2. What Are the Advantages of Life Insurance as a Retirement Plan Investment?

Life insurance, as an investment for retirement plans, affords many advantages. Among these are the following:

(1) Without much doubt, the prime advantage of life insurance as an investment, in the case of any retirement plan, is the assurance that it gives the employee that his investment is safe. In the event of his death, the face amount of the policy will be paid. In the case of any type plan, when the time comes to pay the proceeds of the policy to the employee, the money will be there.

(2) If the employee chooses a monthly payment through an annuity, the life insurance policy will make certain that his profit-sharing account can be changed over to an income for his life, based on the annuity rates which were applicable at the time the original policy was issued.

(3) In the event of the employee's death, the proceeds of the policy will be paid to the beneficiary free of estate tax.

(4) Another worthwhile feature of life insurance lies in the fact that the employee's disability, which might impair his earning ability before his retirement, can be protected against by paying an additional premium to purchase the waiver of premium feature.

(5) By purchasing life insurance as a pension plan investment, the actuarial costs involved in a fixed-benefit type pension plan may be reduced or eliminated, although in a sense the actuarial

145

costs are computed by the insurance company in figuring out the premium to be paid. The insurance company will handle the administration of the pension plan, so that the trustee's cost of administration may be eliminated.

(6) The insurability of the insured, involving the value of the investment, can be protected at the time of purchase.

3. What Disadvantages Are There in Life Insurance as a Retirement Plan Investment?

Life insurance, as a retirement plan investment, has some possible disadvantages. Among them are the following:

(1) The main difficulty with life insurance as a retirement plan investment lies in the low rate of return, as compared with many other types of investments which are available. The return on a life insurance policy will generally be lower than the return that could be obtained on corporate bonds. It will perhaps also be lower than the dividend rate on stocks, and without the inflation hedge which stocks might be said to provide.

(2) There is no possibility of capital gain in the case of life insurance as an investment.

(3) Another adverse feature of life insurance as an investment for retirement plans lies in the fact that the increase in cash value of a life insurance policy is rather slow, and particularly so in the early years of the policy.

(4) A further disadvantage lies in the fact that once the insurance has been purchased, the premiums must be paid each year, whether the corporation has profits or not. There is no flexibility with respect to the payments, although, of course, the corporation might borrow money to pay the premiums and, to the extent of its ability to borrow, there might be some flexibility injected into an insured plan.

In evaluating the advantages and disadvantages of life insurance, as compared with other investments, all of the previously mentioned factors, pro and con, will need to be taken into account. Generally, however, even where life insurance is purchased as a retirement plan investment, it will be balanced off by an auxiliary fund consisting of stocks or bonds, or both, and with a proper balance, the best of both worlds might appear to be possible. It will often be best to utilize insurance in the pension plan or the profit-sharing plan, but, because of its lack of flexibility, perhaps not in both. In a pension plan, particularly of the fixed-benefit type, it would seem desirable to consider protecting the fund, at least during the first five years, with life insurance, so that in the event of the death of one or more of the principal shareholder-employees, the fund would not be wiped out. By investing in life insurance during the early years, the protection of the employees can, to that extent, at least, be assured.

4. What Is the Tax Treatment of Life Insurance When It Is an Investment of the Pension Trust?

In the case of a pension plan, the life insurance purchased as an investment by the trust must be "incidental." It cannot exceed in amount the greater of 100 times the employee's monthly pension or the cash surrender value.[8] Where a pension plan or a profit-sharing plan invests in life insurance, the excess of the face amount of the policy over the amount of the policy reserve constitutes insurance to cover the risk of death. The PS-58 cost of this insurance will be taxable to the employee each year as the premiums are paid, unless the employee himself pays this cost. The PS-58 cost of insurance which is taxed to the employee as paid each year will, in turn, be deductible to the corporation. The amount by which the face amount of the policy exceeds the policy reserve will be free of tax to the beneficiary. The policy reserve will be taxable on the employee's death as long-term capital gain to the beneficiary. Of this reserve, however, $5,000 will not be subject to tax at all where it constitutes the $5,000 death benefit payable by a corporation on the death of an employee. The long-term capital gain taxable to the beneficiary will be reduced by the amount of any contributions by the employee.

The amount of death benefits paid to a beneficiary by a qualified plan is free of estate tax.[9] There has been some discussion of eliminating the estate tax exemption and substituting in its stead the seven-year averaging treatment provided by the Tax Reform Act of 1969 with respect to one-year distributions by pension plans.

---

8 Rev. Rul. 68-31, 1968–1 C.B. 151.
9 Internal Revenue Code, Sec. 2039(c).

How Is Insurance Used in the Professional Corporation?

5. How Is Life Insurance Handled as a Profit-Sharing Plan Investment?

Life insurance can be of value as a profit-sharing plan investment because of the estate tax advantage. On the other hand, by the assignment of all of the incidents of ownership, insurance can, of course, be excluded from the estate of the beneficiary. In the case of a professional corporation, there is much to be said for some investment of the profit-sharing funds in life insurance to protect against the loss to the corporation in the event of the death of any one of the shareholder-employees. Life insurance payable to the profit-sharing trust will serve to benefit the other shareholder-employees in the event of the death of any one of them. In this sense, it would constitute a form of key-man insurance.

Since a profit-sharing plan is essentially a plan to provide for deferred compensation to the employees, it is permissible to invest some of the profit-sharing trust funds in the purchase of life or health insurance. Those purchases must, however, be only "incidental" to the main purpose of the plan. In the case of a profit-sharing plan, the insurance purchased by the plan will be considered incidental, and therefore in compliance with the Internal Revenue Code, if trust funds that have not been accumulated for at least two years are used to pay the premiums and: (1) the premiums paid for life insurance on each participant are less than one-half of the total contributions allocated to him at any particular time, and (2) the plan requires the trustee (a) to convert the entire value of the insurance contract at or before retirement into cash or to provide periodic income so that no portion of such value may be used to continue life insurance protection beyond retirement, or (b) to distribute the contract to the participant at retirement.[10]

6. What About Accident and Health Insurance as a Profit-Sharing Plan Investment?

Where accident and health insurance is purchased as a profit-sharing plan investment, they must, as in the case of life insurance, constitute merely an incidental investment. Where the funds in the profit-sharing trust which are used to purchase the accident and health insurance have not been accumulated for at least two years, the payment of the premiums

---

[10] Rev. Rul. 69-421, 1969–2 C.B. 59, 67.

will be considered incidental, and therefore a justifiable investment, if the premiums used to purchase such accident and health insurance do no exceed 25% of the funds allocated to the account of the participant in question that have not been accumulated for the prescribed period. If the funds are used to buy both ordinary life insurance, as well as accident and health insurance, then the amount paid for the accident and health insurance, plus one-half of the premiums paid for ordinary life insurance, may not, in the aggregate, exceed 25% of the funds allocated to the account of the employee in question.[11]

7. May Existing Policies Be Transferred to the Qualified Plan?

The problems involved in a transfer of existing policies of insurance to a pension or profit-sharing trust are rather difficult. The "transfer for value" problem arises. Under this rule, where an insurance policy is transferred for value, then the proceeds, upon the death of the insured, will constitute taxable income to the extent that they exceed the transfer value and the premiums paid after the transfer, and the tax-free nature of the proceeds will be lost. The transfer for value rule provides that where a life insurance, endowment or annuity contract is transferred for value and the proceeds are paid to the transferee for reasons other than the death of the insured—for example, on surrender, redemption or maturity of the contract—then the transferee will be taxed on the proceeds. If the proceeds are received as an annuity, or in installments for a fixed period, the transferee will compute his tax under the exclusion ratio formula. If the proceeds are received in a lump sum, the transferee will include in his taxable income only such portion of the proceeds in excess of the consideration that he paid for the policy and the income averaging formula, which alleviates tax where the income for one year is in excess of 120% of the average income for the four preceding years, may come into play. The transferee will be allowed to consider as his cost the amount that he paid for the policy, together with any premiums or other consideration that he paid after the time of transfer. Where, however, the transferee's basis is determined by reference to the basis of the transferor, as in the case of a gift or tax-free exchange, then the transfer for value rule will not apply.

The Code permits a policy to be transferred to a corporation in

---

[11] Ibid.

which the insured is a shareholder or officer, or to the insured, his partner or to a partnership in which he is a partner.[12] It does not provide for transfers to a trust. The trust, as a tax-exempt entity, will not be taxable on the receipt of the proceeds. Whether the next step, the payment of the proceeds by the trust to the beneficiary's estate or family, would be tax-free is not at all clear. Had he not transferred the policy to the trust, there would have been no question that the proceeds would be subject to estate tax, but they would not, however, be subject to income tax as well.

Where the insurance policy that is to be considered for transfer to the retirement plan is a term policy and there is no cash value in the policy, it would appear that perhaps the term policy could be transferred to the retirement plan trust without being subject to the transfer for value rule, since a new policy could just as easily be issued, as to transfer an existing policy to the pension or profit-sharing trust. There are, however, no published rulings or cases on the point. If this could be safely done, it could be helpful, where the preservation of insurability may be of importance to the insured, since he might, since issuance of the policy, have become uninsurable. In the case of a policy which has cash value, however, at this time it would appear unwise, in the absence of further clarification by the Service or the courts, to transfer an existing policy to a retirement plan, since one cannot determine that it complies with the express language of the Code, which specifies only certain transferees to whom a policy can be transferred, without running into the problem of the transfer for value. Further problems arise with respect to the transfer of existing policies, in that they may not comply with the requirements of a qualified plan, particularly those relating to annuity provisions and the requirement that the life insurance benefits be merely "incidental."

C. Group Insurance

A corporation may purchase group term life insurance for the benefit of its employees, taking a deduction for the payments, without making such payments taxable to the employee or his beneficiaries, to the extent that the coverage for the employee does not exceed $50,000. The possibility of acquiring group term life insurance is certainly one of the major benefits

---

[12] Internal Revenue Code, Sec. 101(a)(2).

involved in forming a professional corporation, since group term life insurance purchased by a partnership cannot provide these benefits to the partners. While group term policies generally require at least ten people to be covered, a smaller professional group might very well be able to acquire some form of group term life insurance through participation in a trade association group contract, even though the particular professional corporation might have only one or two employees.

Group term life insurance has non-tax advantages which are quite real and valuable to a professional corporation. It permits coverage of employees in many cases without their being required to have physical examinations to prove their insurability. In addition, the cost of group term life insurance is generally considerably less than individual term policies.

1. What Are the Income Tax Consequences for the Employee and His Beneficiaries?

Group term policies involve favorable income tax considerations for both the employee during his lifetime and for his beneficiaries under the group term policy after his death.

(a) *For the Employee*

The employee will not be required to include in his taxable income the cost of group term life insurance purchased by his employer, to the extent that the face value of the policy for him does not exceed $50,000.[13] To the extent that the face value of the policy exceeds $50,000, the cost of such excess will be taxed to the employee. Generally, however, the cost of such excess insurance will only be about one-half the amount that it would cost the employee to buy such coverage himself on a term basis. In addition, if the employee has terminated his employment and has reached retirement age or is disabled, then the $50,000 limit will not apply.

(b) *For the Beneficiary*

The amount received under a group term policy by the beneficiary does not constitute taxable income to the beneficiary, where the amounts are paid by reason of the death of the insured.[14] It does not matter whether

---

[13] Internal Revenue Code, Sec. 79(a)(1).
[14] Internal Revenue Code, Sec. 101(a)(1).

the amount payable to the beneficiary is paid in a lump sum or in installments. Where the policy has been transferred for value, the exclusion from gross income of the policy proceeds will be limited to the consideration paid for the policy, and the premiums that were thereafter paid by the transferee, unless the transferee is a partner of the insured, a partnership of which he was a member or a corporation in which he was a stockholder or officer.

Where the proceeds of the policy are retained by the insurance company under a settlement policy, or in some other manner, the interest paid by the insurance company will be taxed to the beneficiary. If, however, the beneficiary is the spouse of the insured, then interest earned on the amount held by the insurance company will be free of tax to such spouse up to an amount of $1,000 per year.[15]

2. What Are the Estate Tax Consequences?

Group term life insurance, like other forms of life insurance, is includable in the taxable estate of the insured if it is payable to the insured's gross estate, or if he has retained any of the incidents of ownership in the policy, exercisable either by himself alone or in conjunction with any other person. Among those rights would be the right to change the beneficiary, or to have the proceeds revert to his estate, if such reversionary interest is more than 5%.

(a) *May the Policy Escape Estate Tax Through Assignment?*

If the ownership of the policy may be assigned by the insured, this opens a way to have the proceeds of the policy escape estate tax upon his death. May the insured assign his interest in a group policy on his life? In considering this question, it must be noted that the policy is not just a policy on him alone. It is a group policy.

The Internal Revenue Service, in two rulings,[16] has held that if both the state law and the group policy give the employee a right to assign the policy and he does so, and he could not have effected a cancellation of the coverage by terminating his employment, then the policy proceeds, on his death, will not be subject to estate tax. Forty states now provide for such

---

[15] Internal Revenue Code, Sec. 101(d)(1).
[16] Rev. Rul. 68-334, 1968-1 C.B. 403; Rev. Rul. 69-54, 1969-1 C.B. 221.

an assignment. In two cases the courts have approved such transfers of group policies.[17]

In seeking to assign a group term policy, it will be essential, in each case, to review carefully the provisions of the state law, with respect to such an assignment, and the provisions of the group policy itself. In the case of a one-man corporation, or a corporation with very few shareholders, there may still be some effort on the part of the Service to hold that if the insured had the right to terminate the policy, by terminating his employment, this could be an incident of ownership which would cause the proceeds of the policy to be included in his taxable estate, even though he had gone through the formality of assigning the policy to someone else. Where the policy has been paid for with community funds, it will be important to make sure that the spouse of the insured has participated in the assignment, where the assignment is to someone other than the spouse of the insured.

Another problem arises with respect to the contemplation of death question. The Service holds that to the extent that any premiums were paid by the insured within three years of his death, then the portion of the policy proceeds represented by such premiums should be included in his taxable estate. The Service still adheres to a ruling to this effect,[18] although it has been repudiated in a number of recent Court decisions,[19] even though it has been criticized as an effort to restore the "premium payment test" with respect to life insurance. Under that test, which was eliminated by Section 2042 of the Code, life insurance proceeds were taxed in the estate of the insured where he paid the premiums on the policy.

The Service has recently ruled [20] that a group policy that includes permanent insurance, paid up value or equivalent benefit, must include all the employees in the same class.

---

[17] Landorf, 408 F.2d 461 (Ct. Cls., 1969); Estate of Max J. Gorby, 53 T.C. 80 (1969), Acq. IRB 1970-18.
[18] Rev. Rul. 67-463, 1967-2 C.B. 327.
[19] First National Bank of Midland v. U.S., 423 F.2d 1286 (CA5, 1970); Gorman v. U.S., 288 F. Supp, 225 (DC. Mich., 1968); Coleman v. Comm'r, 52 T.C. 921 (1969).
[20] T.D. 7132.

How Is Insurance Used in the Professional Corporation?

D. Key-Man and Split-Dollar Insurance

Two other principal types of insurance may be considered for a professional corporation. These are key-man and split-dollar insurance. Split-dollar insurance is essentially key-man insurance, purchased in a special way, with the corporation paying part of the premiums and the employee paying the balance.

1. Key-Man Insurance

In the case of key-man insurance the premiums are not deductible by the corporation, but the proceeds from the policy are not taxable when received. Quite often key-man insurance is purchased to fund a stock purchase agreement, or to provide deferred compensation. It may also be purchased by the corporation to provide death benefits on the death of the employee. It is a form of term insurance. In some cases, the corporation will purchase the policy and later transfer it to the employee or sell it to him. In other instances, the key man may already have the policy, having taken it out and paid the premiums. He now wishes to transfer the policy to the corporation, or perhaps sell it to the corporation. Such a transfer will not constitute a transfer for value under the Code. Since the loss of a key man is a matter of some importance to a corporation, the purpose of the insurance may in fact be to provide it with funds to replace a key man whose services are of substantial value and who cannot be replaced without considerable expense.

2. Split-Dollar Insurance

In the case of split-dollar insurance, the policy generally involves payment by the corporation of a portion of the premiums equal to the increase in cash value of the policy each year. The employee will pay the balance of the premiums. The corporation will be the beneficiary, to the extent of the cash surrender value of the policy, and the employee will designate the beneficiaries to receive the balance of the policy proceeds. The employee is taxed each year on the difference between what he pays in premiums and what he would have paid for term insurance on the excess insurance coverage which is being provided for him by the corporation through its payment of premiums. Split-dollar insurance can be utilized where there may not be a sufficient number of employees to qualify for a group plan, or if a group plan would be too expensive. The split-dollar insurance may be a means of providing an employee with a larger amount of insurance than he could provide out of his own funds during the period of his employment.

A practice of borrowing against the cash value of the policy, in the case of split-dollar insurance, was severely restricted by the adoption of Section 264 of the Code, which denies a deduction where the policy has been purchased through borrowing against the cash value until it can be shown that at least four of the first seven annual premium payments have been paid without the use of borrowed funds.

The effect of split-dollar life insurance is to separate the investment portion of the policy from the risk of death portion. The corporation pays for the former, and the employee pays for the latter. As a result, it permits the employee to obtain greater coverage, and perhaps later on acquire from the employer the investment portion of the policy as well. In the meantime, he has had the benefit of the greater coverage, without having to pay for all of the premiums himself.

E. How Will the Insurance Plans Be Coordinated?

Because of the unique nature of insurance as an investment, providing the funds which are needed and at the time needed, whether the insurance be life insurance, casualty insurance, health and accident or some other type of insurance, it becomes most important to have all of the insurance programs involved in a professional corporation situation well-coordinated. In Chapter 2 the role of insurance in funding the stock purchase agreement, in the event of the death of a shareholder, has been noted. In this chapter, the role of insurance as an investment of the retirement trust has been considered at length. In virtually every case, each of the shareholder-employees of the professional corporation will, if insurable, have his own personal life insurance program.

1. Should Ownership of Some Policies Be Transferred?

The shareholder-employee will need to give careful consideration to the possibility of excluding from his taxable estate life insurance on his life by transferring ownership of the policy, whether to his wife or to other members of his family. If he feels that he can get along without using the life insurance policies as collateral on loans and if he feels that the insurance program of the corporation provides adequate protection, together with other investments, for his estate, both as to taxes and expenses of administration, then he might well decide, at least on certain policies, to transfer ownership once and for all to someone other than himself and thereby reduce his taxable estate. All of this, of course, will require careful planning, not only with his life underwriter, but with his counsel and Certified Public Accountant as well.

2. What Is the Role of Personally Owned Life Insurance?

The counsel for the corporation, in working with the life underwriter, as well as with the officers and Board of Directors of the professional corporation, will need to consider the role of the personal life insurance programs of the shareholder-employees. As each shareholder-employee evaluates his own life insurance program, and particularly the cash needed to pay premiums each year, he will need to consider the total amount of coverage on his life, including the group life insurance carried by the corporation, the insurance purchased by the pension trust and the profit-sharing trust, as well as his own personal life insurance, both ordinary life and term.

3. Should Some Policies Be Converted to Paid-Up Insurance?

In some cases, it may well be that the acquisition of the group life insurance by the corporation, as well as the investment in life insurance through the retirement plan, together with disability insurance, may lead the shareholder-employee to conclude that he could afford to convert some of his personal life insurance to paid-up insurance, thereby saving not only the cost of some of the premiums, but the tax which he has to pay on the income which he has to earn in order to provide the after-tax money for the premiums. In other words, as a result of the group life insurance and the retirement plan insurance, he may feel that his family has adequate protection against the danger of his death, so that he can perhaps afford to put some of the premium money into other types of investments, or to relieve his cash needs for personal expenditures, such as education of his children, travel and other expenditures, either for investment or personal satisfaction.

How Is Insurance Used in the Professional Corporation?

For the shareholder-employee to reach a conclusion on these matters without careful and adequate discussion with his own attorney and life underwriter would be shortsighted. Accordingly, a careful review of the entire insurance program will be in order for each shareholder-employee in light of the changed picture which has resulted from the incorporation of the professional enterprise and the acquisition, in connection therewith, of substantial amounts of life insurance coverage in tax-deductible form.

7

How Do You Operate
the Corporation?

Once the professional corporation has been duly organized, in accordance with the state statute, and all the instruments needed to make it a proper and formal corporation under state law have been duly executed, the question arises as to how you are to operate the corporation. In operating the corporation, are there tax problems which will inhibit or limit the use of the corporation as a tax shelter? Limitations on the use of the corporation may arise in a number of different ways.

There are five provisions of the Internal Revenue Code which may be brought into play by the Internal Revenue Service in attacking the operation of the corporation, even though the corporation was duly and formally organized and is a valid professional corporation. Cases interpreting each of these provisions of the Code may be brought into play by the Service to sustain its position that the corporation, while properly organized, nevertheless should not be taxed on the income involved and that the income should, in fact, be taxed to the professional shareholder, or there should be an extra tax.

The sections of the Code which may be brought into play by the Service will be discussed in the following order:

(1) *Section 61.* This section sets forth the general definition of gross income. In applying this section, the Service will contend that

the income involved is the taxable gross income of the individual shareholder-employee, rather than that of the professional corporation.

(2) *Section 482.* This section relates to the allocation of income and deductions among taxpayers. It permits the Service to allocate among taxpayers income and deductions when the Service determines that this is necessary in order to prevent evasion of taxes or clearly reflect the income of such taxpayers.

(3) *Section 269.* This section relates to acquisitions made to evade or avoid income tax. It applies where any person acquires control of a corporation or the property of a corporation for the principal purpose of evasion or avoidance of income tax.

(4) *Section 541.* This section relates to the personal holding company tax. It permits the Service to invoke a 70% tax on the undistributed personal holding income of a corporation if 60% or more of its income is derived from certain types of passive income, including income derived from personal service contracts.

(5) *Section 531.* This section imposes a surtax on corporations improperly accumulating surplus. The tax is 27½% on the first $100,000 of accumulated taxable income and 38½% beyond that figure, in addition to the regular income tax, if the corporation was formed or availed of for the purpose of avoiding the income tax of its shareholders.

A. May the Service Tax the Corporate Income to the Shareholders Under Section 61 and the Roubik Case?

Without much question, the most important tax case with respect to professional corporations after the publication of TIR 1019 on August 8, 1969, in which the Service stated that it would no longer litigate the question of whether professional corporations and associations, properly organized under state statutes, would be taxable as corporations, was the Tax Court case of *Jerome J. Roubik v. Comm'r.*[1] This case stands for the proposition that not only must a professional corporation be properly organized under the state statute, it must, in addition, be operated as a corporation.

---

[1] Jerome J. Roubik v. Comm'r, 53 T.C. 365 (1969).

How Do You Operate the Corporation?

It must not be a mere bookkeeping device to give the professional share-holders the tax benefits of a corporation, without operating the corporation as such. The *Roubik* case has made believers of any who would lightly set up a professional corporation and then assume that just by setting up the corporate entity, they would automatically obtain all of the benefits of a corporation for Federal tax purposes, even though they did not adhere to the corporate form in conducting their professional practice.

1. What Did the Corporate Owners in Roubik Do?

In the *Roubik* case, four radiologists in Wisconsin organized a professional corporation in accordance with the Service Corporation Law of Wisconsin. They became shareholders, adopted a pension plan and each entered into a written employment agreement with the corporation, which was called Pfeffer Associates. The corporation opened a checking account and all the fees earned by each radiologist were deposited in the account. A bookkeeper kept records to show the income of each owner and the expenses of his practice which were paid by the corporation. The doctors continued to conduct their practice under their own names in exactly the same manner as they had done before. Each doctor kept his own office and his own equipment. He had his own employees and they worked for him. Each of them billed his patients on his own forms.

2. What Did the Tax Court Hold?

The Tax Court held that the question involved was not one as to whether the corporation was to be classified as a corporation for Federal income tax purposes, but rather whether the corporation "earned" the income which was involved. The Court held that the income was not earned by the corporation, but that it was earned by the individual shareholders. It concluded that the income, therefore, should be taxed to the doctors, and not the corporation, citing an earlier Tax Court case, *Richard Rubin*,[2] for the proposition that where a corporation provides personal services for a fee, the income is earned by whoever has the "ultimate direction and control" over the earning of the compensation. The Court, in the *Roubik* case, concluded that the corporation was never given any control over the professional activities of the doctors who were its shareholder-employees.

---

[2] Richard Rubin v. Comm'r, 51 T.C. 251 (1968).

How Do You Operate the Corporation?

The Court stated that the doctors did nothing more than centralize their bookkeeping; that they could not, while separately engaged in their professional practice, become employees of the corporation through the purely formal device of incorporating a set of bookkeeping sheets. The Court observed further that the various professional corporation statutes did not relieve the professional corporation of the obligation of performing some meaningful business function in order to be recognized as a separate entity for tax purposes; and that the corporation must be given substance through the manner in which it actually operates. The Court concluded that the taxpayers did not "put flesh on the bones of the corporate skeleton, irrespective of the question of its legal existence under local law." Accordingly, the Court held that the corporation would not be recognized as a corporation for Federal income tax purposes.

3. May the Service Rely on Section 61?

The basis of the *Roubik* decision was the "sham corporation" argument; that while the corporation might have been properly organized, nevertheless, in its operation, it was nothing but a sham. The Tax Court in its *Roubik* opinion did not cite any section of the Code, but it did cite its earlier *Rubin* decision. The *Rubin* decision in the Tax Court relied expressly on Section 61 of the Code. Accordingly, it may be assumed that this was, therefore, the section of the Code relied upon by the Court in *Roubik*. The *Rubin* case, however, after the Tax Court's decision in *Roubik*, was, on appeal to the Second Circuit Court of Appeals, reversed and remanded to the Tax Court.[3] The Circuit Court expressly rejected the application of Section 61 of the Code and directed that the facts be considered in the light of Section 482 of the Code. This latter section permits the Service to allocate income or deductions, where necessary to properly reflect taxable income of different taxpayers.

4. What Did the Circuit Court Hold in the Rubin Case as to Section 61?

In the *Rubin* case, the facts are, briefly, that Rubin obtained an option to buy control of Dorman Mills, a textile corporation. Then he and

---

[3] Rubin v. Comm'r, 429 F.2d 650 (C.A. 2, 1970).

his brothers organized another corporation, Park, in which he owned 70% of the stock. Then Park and Dorman Mills entered into a contract under which Rubin was to manage Dorman Mills. The management fees were paid by Dorman Mills to Park. The Tax Court held that the fees should be taxed to Rubin since, under Section 61, they were income of Rubin, rather than of Park, his controlled corporation. The Tax Court, in so holding, noted that it was not attacking the validity of Park as a corporation, but rather attacking the validity of transactions purportedly entered into by Park. It concluded that, as a matter of substance, Rubin worked directly for Dorman Mills, and the income paid by Dorman Mills to Park was income which had been earned by Rubin; it, therefore, should be taxable to him. The Court cited an old Supreme Court decision, *Lucas v. Earl* [4] in which the Supreme Court had held that income which had been assigned by the one who earned it should, despite the assignment, be taxed to the one who earned the income. The Tax Court pointed out that Rubin clearly directed and controlled the earning of the income. The Circuit Court, however, in considering the matter on appeal, held that Section 61, the section defining gross income, was not the proper section to apply, and remanded the case to the Tax Court to consider the question under Section 482. On remand,[5] the Tax Court, in *Rubin*, held that Section 482 did apply and could be used to prevent a distortion of income where the employee was not merely an employee, but was in the business of providing management services.

B. May the Service Allocate the Income of a Professional Corporation to the Shareholders Under Section 482?

The Circuit Court of Appeals in the *Rubin* case took the position that the broad sweep of Section 61 of the Code, defining "gross income," should not be relied upon where the facts permitted the determination of the question under a more specific section of the Code—namely, Section 482. Section 482 is the section permitting the Service to allocate income and deductions between taxpayers when the Service determines that this is

---

[4] Lucas v. Earl, 281 U.S. 111 (1930).
[5] Richard Rubin v. Comm'r, 56 T.C. ——— (1971), relying on Borge v. Comm'r, 405 F.2d 573 (C.A. 2, 1968) and Pauline W. Ach, 358 F.2d 342 (C.A. 6, 1966).

necessary to reflect income of the taxpayers properly. The Court noted that by applying Section 482 there would be greater flexibility in determining the question, rather than deciding it on the "all-or-nothing approach" of the Tax Court.

The Circuit Court's decision in *Rubin* raises the interesting question of whether the Court would have reversed the Tax Court's decision in *Roubik* for the same reason were the *Roubik* facts before it for decision. In other words, should the *Roubik* case have been decided on the basis of Section 482, the allocation of income provision, rather than on the broad basis of Section 61, the gross income definition section? The Tax Court's decision on remand of *Rubin* clearly indicates it would apply Section 482.

Does this mean that the *Roubik* decision is no longer to be followed in its application to professional corporations? While it is likely that the question may well be raised at some time in the future, it would certainly not seem wise for any professional group, in operating its corporation, to permit itself to fall into the predicament in which the taxpayers in the *Roubik* case found themselves. The moral of the *Roubik* case certainly appears to be that not only must a professional corporation be properly organized as such under the applicable state statute, it must, in addition, be operated as a corporation. The shareholder-employees would be unwise to make themselves the guinea pigs for further consideration of this question, either in the Tax Court or a Circuit Court of Appeals, if they can avoid it by reading the road signs set out in *Roubik*.

C. May Section 269 Apply to a Professional Corporation Situation?

While the possibility of application to professional corporations of Section 269, the tax avoidance section of the Code, permitting the Service to attack corporate acquisitions on the ground of tax avoidance, has been often mentioned, no case has yet arisen in which that section has been applied to professional corporations.

1. Isn't Section 269 Only Applicable to "Loss Corporations"?

Section 269 has generally been applied to situations where control of a "tax loss" corporation was acquired by another corporation in order to offset the tax losses of the acquired corporation against the taxable income of the acquiring corporation. Nevertheless, the section represents another string to the bow in the arsenal of the Service in attacking transfers of controlled corporations or their property, where tax avoidance can be shown by the Service to be a principal purpose of the transaction. Whether the formation of a professional corporation would be considered the acquisition of control of a corporation for the purpose of securing the benefit of tax deductions under Section 269 still remains to be determined. The Chief Counsel of the Service has indicated that he, himself, has some serious doubt as to whether Section 269 would properly apply to the formation of a professional corporation.[6]

Whether Section 269 can be applied to professional corporations, or whether it will be applied by the Service in the future, it certainly should be kept in mind by those organizing and operating professional corporations that the professional corporation should not be considered by them to be a convenient tax avoidance device. It needs to have business purpose, as well as tax purpose. The same lesson to be learned from the *Roubik* decision applies to Section 269; namely, that the shareholders of the professional corporation should not only see that the corporation is properly organized, but that it should operate as a corporation, rather than as a mere bookkeeping device, which proves convenient to reduce taxes. The business advantages of the corporation should be carefully considered and kept in mind by the shareholders.

2. Does Section 269 Apply to a Professional Corporation if Tax Purposes Are a Major Factor?

In considering the possible application of Section 269 to professional corporations, it should be noted that even though the business purposes justifying the existence of the corporation may be not too important, when compared with the tax advantages of the professional corporation, the predominance of the tax purposes would not justify the imposition of Section 269. The Code permits a taxpayer to select the form of business organization in which he will operate, whether in the form of a proprietorship, a partnership or a corporation. The tax treatment of each of them will differ and that is a matter of individual decision for the taxpayer. The taxpayer

---

[6] J. Martin Worthy, "IRS Chief Counsel Outlines What Lies Ahead for Professional Corporations," 32, *The Journal of Taxation* (Feb. 1970), 88, 90.

is also in a position to change from one form to the other, even though the primary purpose for such change is based on tax considerations. Accordingly, an effort on the part of the Service to apply Section 269 to a professional corporation situation would seem unjustified and unlikely.

In a factual situation as extreme as that in the *Roubik* case, were the Service to rely on Section 269, rather than Section 61 or Section 482, there would appear to be at least some possibility, if not probability, that the Service might, on such strong facts, be able to sustain its position. Certainly the use of Section 269, rather than Section 61, might well have been considered by the Service on the facts which were present in the *Roubik* case. The application of Section 269, as a rather broad provision, at least broader than Section 482, would appear to be open to the same objections the Second Circuit found to Section 61 in the *Rubin* case. It does appear, however, that the taxpayers in *Roubik*, by doing so little to operate as a corporation, certainly left themselves open to attack on any of the three different statutory provisions, whether it be Section 61, Section 482 or Section 269.

The Chief Counsel of the Internal Revenue Service has himself indicated that even though a corporation was organized principally for the purpose of taking advantage of Code provisions relating to qualified pension and profit-sharing plans, there would be some question whether such a purpose would constitute "evasion or avoidance" of taxes for purposes of Section 269.[7] In taking such a position, the Chief Counsel noted that the Code provisions with respect to pension and profit-sharing plans represented a deliberate action of Congress in granting certain tax benefits to employers and employees. These purposes would appear to take priority over a broad section such as Section 269, which has, for the most part, been confined to the acquisition of loss corporations.

3. How Can the Shareholders Protect Themselves?

In operating the corporation, it will be important for the shareholder-employees to pay attention to the business purposes, as well as the tax purposes for the corporation. If they think of the corporation merely

---

[7] See Footnote 4, *supra*.

as a means of cutting down taxes, they will be neglecting some very important benefits to be derived from the corporate form of organization, which may not be related to taxes at all. In some cases, it may take a little time for them to operate through a Board of Directors and officers, with appropriate minutes and corporate resolutions, but there will be purely business advantages from so operating which will become more evident as the organization goes ahead with its operation of the business in corporate form, and with the centralized management which that affords. The professional corporation is not just a tax avoidance "gimmick," and it will be well for the shareholder-employees to think of the business purposes of the corporation as they proceed with its operation.

4. How Can a Corporate Advisor Make Sure the Corporation Will Be Properly Operated?

How can an advisor help the shareholders avoid the pitfall of the radiologists in the *Roubik* case? One technique that can be applied is to set up a schedule of steps to be taken, particularly toward the close of the first fiscal year of the corporation. At that point, certain matters can be checked to make sure that they have been completed and followed through to their conclusion.

The points to check at year-end are as follows: (1) The minute book should be up to date, with the minutes signed. (2) The stock certificates should be issued and proper record made in the stock certificate book. (3) The bank account should be in the corporate name and the appropriate bank resolutions for signing of checks and for loans should have been adopted. (4) All appropriate tax returns, Federal and state, should be properly filed and on time. (5) Insurance payments should be made by the corporation where appropriate. (6) All corporate accounting records and withholding taxes should be handled by the corporation. This latter must be started in the first quarter of the corporation's activity. Withholding on the salaries of the shareholder-employees is of particular importance. Withholding on the salaries of other employees will merely be carried over from the predecessor partnership or proprietorship. (7) All the property which is to be transferred to the corporation should be properly documented, including leases and other instruments in connection with the property involved. By use of a checklist, full compliance with all of the details required can be quickly established. In this way a practical solution can be found to the question, "How can the operation of the corporation as a corporation be proven to the satisfaction of the Service?"

D. Is the Professional Corporation Vulnerable to Attack as a Personal Holding Company?

Under Section 541 of the Code, personal holding company income includes income from a contract under which the corporation is to furnish personal services, if some person other than the corporation has the right to designate the individual who is to perform the services. Accordingly, if a professional corporation enters into a contract, for example, with a patient who has the right to designate the particular doctor who is to perform the services involved, then the income received by the professional corporation from the patient will become personal holding company income. If 60% or more of the income of the corporation is made up of personal holding company income, then the 70% personal holding company surtax will apply to the undistributed personal holding company income.

1. How Can the Personal Holding Company Provisions Be Avoided?

In order to be a personal holding company, the stock of the corporation must be owned by not more than five individuals, so this problem would not arise where there are more than five stockholders. In determining the number of shareholders, stock which is owned by a shareholder, either directly or indirectly, is considered to be owned by the particular shareholder. Another escape from the personal holding company is found in a provision [8] which states that the personal service contract provision does not apply unless the particular individual owns 25% or more in value of the stock of the corporation.

The answer to the personal holding company question for a professional corporation will generally be determined by the manner in which the corporation operates. If there are contracts with patients or clients

---

[8] Internal Revenue Code, Sec. 543(a)(7).

who can designate which particular professional individual will perform the services involved, then a personal holding company problem could very well exist. By making sure that the control as to who will perform the services rests in the corporation, rather than in the patient or the client, the question can be eliminated.

In the case of a large professional group, the personal holding company problem will be eliminated by the stock ownership provision of Section 541, since there may be more than five stockholders and the provision may also be made inapplicable with respect to personal service contract income by the fact that no particular individual owns 25% or more of the stock. Where, however, there are less than five stockholders, the question might be raised. In most such cases, however, the professional corporation will, as a matter of course, retain the right to designate the employee who will perform the services. Certainly the execution of a contract giving the patient or client the right to designate the individual who will perform the services would be rather unusual. It will be important, in operating the corporation, however, to make certain that the patient or client is not in any way given an indication that he will be in a position to designate the particular individual who will perform the services. Where written contracts with clients or patients are involved, it would be well for the contract to contain a provision preserving the right of the corporation to designate the individual who will perform the services.

2. How About the One-Man Corporation?

The problem of a personal holding company in the case of a one-man professional corporation is obviously more complicated than for a professional corporation which includes several shareholders. A nice problem of semantics may become involved. Is it the corporation or the shareholder who has the right to determine who will perform the services? When the patient or client comes in to receive professional services, is there any real way that the right of the corporation to designate who will perform the services can be asserted? Each case will need to be considered on its own facts. Certainly the possibility of a contention by the Service that the one-man professional corporation is a personal holding company should be carefully considered. Steps should be taken to make sure that the corporation does, in fact, retain the right to designate the professional individual who will perform the services, whether that be the sole shareholder himself, or some other qualified professional designated by the corporation.

3. Why Not Pay Out All the Earnings and Profits?

A simple solution for the personal holding company problem in the case of the one-man corporation, as well as in cases where there are several shareholders, will be to make sure that no earnings are retained in the corporation. There has been some thought that if all of the corporate profits are paid out in the form of salaries, bonuses and contributions to retirement plans, as well as for fringe benefits, the corporation will not have any business purpose and therefore might be attacked as a sham. Generally some profit will be retained in the corporation, so to that extent, the argument of the sham corporation will be refuted. If, however, even though virtually no profit is retained in the corporation, the corporation in fact operates as a corporation, observing all of the formalities of corporate operation, including holding of meetings, keeping of minutes, adopting resolutions and acting through a centralized management, the danger of the personal holding company attack would seem very remote at best.

Retaining profits in the corporation will not be necessary in the case of most professional corporations, since the amount of capital investment needed for the operation of the corporation is not large. Sound planning for the professional corporation would appear to dictate the retention of only a small amount of profits in the corporation at the end of the corporate year. In the case of professional corporations which need very substantial equipment, for example radiology or pathology equipment in the case of a medical clinic, these can be leased from some other entity which owns them. The same can be done with the real estate which is occupied by the clinic. Sound planning, in the case of the professional corporation, and in light of all the facts, will be justified. As far as the personal holding company question is involved, it would seem prudent not to attempt to retain any substantial amount of corporate profits in the corporation. If capital equipment is needed, then careful computation should be made near the end of the corporate year to determine what deductions are available through depreciation on such equipment, so that a calculation of the amount needed to be paid out in bonuses and contributions to the retirement plan, as well as for fringe benefits, can be exactly determined. When this has been done, the amount left in the corporation will not be sufficiently large to make a personal holding company attack on the corporation worthwhile for the Internal Revenue Service to consider.

4. How About a Dividend to the Stockholders?

There is a further relief provision from the personal holding company tax in that the corporation can pay out the personal holding company income to the shareholders in the form of bonuses, to the extent that this is within the limit of reasonable compensation, and the balance will constitute dividends taxable to the shareholders as such. Such income will be still subject to a double tax, once to the corporation and again to the shareholder, but the added personal holding company tax will thereby be avoided.

E. Will the Section 531 Surtax on Unreasonable Accumulations Apply?

One of the prime advantages of a professional corporation appears to lie in the opportunity to accumulate income in the corporation, subject only to a 22% corporate rate of tax, as long as the corporate income is not in excess of $25,000 each year.

1. Should the Corporation Pay Tax on Some Taxable Income?

Many writers have advised that the corporation should pay tax each year on some income, more than a nominal amount, in order to establish the validity and authenticity of the corporation as an entity, separate and apart from the professional shareholders. Unfortunately, however, if the accumulations exceed $100,000 of earnings and profits, then the surtax on unreasonable accumulation of earnings and profits under Section 531 of the Code will apply. This tax is in addition to the ordinary corporate tax. The only alternative will be for the corporation to distribute its earnings to the shareholders, but once the income has been accumulated in the corporation, subject to the 22% tax of the corporation, then this will need to be added to the top bracket of the individual shareholder in order to determine the total tax ultimately to be paid on such income. At this point, the tax savings brought about by the receipt of income at a 22% rate will not look nearly as good as it did at the outset.

How Do You Operate the Corporation?

2. What Are Reasonable Needs in the Case of a Professional Corporation?

A corporation can, of course, be protected against the charge of unreasonable accumulation of earnings and profits to the extent that the corporation can justify the accumulation for legitimate corporate needs, such as the acquisition of property needed in the operation of the business. Ordinarily, the state statute authorizing professional corporations will permit investment only in property which is reasonably required for the operation of the professional activities of the corporation. Outside investments will generally not be permitted. Property for which accumulations of profits may be made will generally include professional equipment, office space, debt payments, as well as life insurance on key men. A reasonable amount of operating capital will, of course, also justify the accumulation of earnings and profits.

3. How About Accumulations for Redemption of Stock?

The accumulation of earnings and profits for the purpose of redeeming stock, for purposes of Section 303 of the Code (that is, a redemption of stock to pay death taxes), is now permitted under Section 537 of the Code as a reasonable need of the business. The redemption of the stock with the proceeds of life insurance purchased for such purpose will be adequate justification for the investment in the policy and the redemption will not be taxed as a dividend. In the case of a professional corporation, since redemption of a shareholder's stock is an integral and important feature of the professional corporation, the accumulation of earnings and profits in order to prepare for such redemption will be considered a valid purpose of accumulation of earnings and profits.

Often the statute providing for professional corporations will contain a provision requiring the redemption of a shareholder's stock upon his death. Under the Tax Reform Act of 1969, Section 537 of the Code was amended to provide expressly for redemption of stock as a reasonable need of a business. On the other hand, in the case of a professional corporation, its scope of activities is basically limited to the practice of the profession and the acquisition of such property as is reasonably needed to facilitate such practice. This would seem to preclude arguments which are generally available to ordinary corporations, that they have other business needs for the accumulation, such as need for expansion, and acquisition of related and subsidiary businesses. Accordingly, the use of a professional corporation as a tax shelter for the accumulation of earnings and profits turns out not to be as good an idea as it might have appeared at first blush.

F.   How Should the Corporation Be Operated?

In summary, it might be concluded that those undertaking to form a professional corporation should be fully aware of its limitations. Not only must it be properly organized, but also it must be properly operated. While it affords many advantages, there can be pitfalls, as the taxpayers in the *Roubik* decision found out. The Internal Revenue Service has many weapons in its arsenal and will be ready to use them whenever it concludes that the professional corporation is being utilized to obtain tax advantages alone and is not being operated as a corporation, but only as a device to save taxes. The Service has a choice of several statutory provisions and a host of tax cases backing up each section. For those, however, who abide by the rules, there would appear to be no great danger from attack on any of these statutory grounds, since the Service has clearly indicated that professional corporations, properly organized and properly operated, in accordance with the state statute involved, will be recognized by the Service.

It might be helpful to set forth briefly a list of the principal areas in which, in operating the corporation, the fact that the corporation is a real entity and not just a means of reducing the taxes of the shareholder-employees, may be established. These will be the indicia of a true corporate activity, rather than a bookkeeping device. By applying these tests, one can quickly establish that the corporation is not only a corporation under state law, but also operates as such and therefore should be recognized by the Service.

1. *Banking.* All bank accounts should be kept in the name of the corporation and any borrowing should be done by the corporation.
2. *Billing.* All fees should be made payable to the corporation, and the statements to patients and clients should be sent out under the corporate name.

173

3. *Letterheads.* All letterheads should bear the name of the corporation and the corporate name should be also used in any telephone book or other listings which are professionally acceptable, as well as on professional cards and the principal place of business of the corporation.

4. *Tax Returns.* All tax returns, Federal, state and local, should be filed in the name of the corporation. Where withholding of tax is called for, it should be done by the corporation. Withholding of income tax and Social Security tax should be done in the name of the corporation. Franchise and local taxes should be paid by the corporation.

5. *Leases.* All real estate utilized by the corporation should be leased in the corporate name and contracts should be executed in the name of the corporation.

6. *Insurance.* Insurance policies for malpractice insurance, disability, group life, hospitalization, key-man, liability, casualty and automobile insurance should be carried in the name of the corporation and the premiums should be paid by the corporation.

7. *Supplies.* All supplies and, to the extent feasible, equipment also, should be purchased by the corporation, although equipment owned by others should be leased by the corporation and the corporation should pay the rent thereon.

8. *Employment Contracts.* There should be written employment contracts between the corporation and all shareholder-employees, and, with other employees as well, where written contracts may be in order.

9. *Expenses.* All expenses related to the operation of the corporation should be paid by the corporation itself, rather than by the shareholder-employees. In no case should the corporation ever pay expenses which are personal to the shareholder-employees, rather than being valid business expenses of the corporation itself.

10. *Board of Directors.* The corporation should have an active and functioning Board of Directors, together with an Executive Committee, if that is feasible, and they should actively control the operation of the corporation, together with the officers, and their

actions should be duly authenticated by the minute book of the corporation.

G. Who Will Do the Job?

If the professional corporation will follow the above ten rules it will be operating properly as a corporation and should have no difficulty in being recognized as such by the Internal Revenue Service. In accomplishing this, the corporation will have need of qualified and responsible accountants, who will see to the filing of tax returns and keep track of the financial affairs of the corporation through the preparation of proper accounting data and financial statements. In the case of a professional corporation which is engaged in operating a medical clinic, the importance of employing a competent clinic manager cannot be over-emphasized. Any clinic with more than three doctors will generally find that employment of a competent clinic manager will prove to be a good investment. The services of a competent life underwriter will be needed in connection with the various life insurance programs of the professional corporation and competent professional advice will be needed with respect to other types of insurance. The retirement plans will require proper administration and, where actuarial computations are involved, professional actuaries will be not only helpful, but essential. In handling the investments of the retirement trusts, the help of competent investment advisors, whether the funds be invested in securities or in life insurance, will be essential. Last but not least, will be proper legal counsel to see that all the legal aspects of the corporate operation are carried out in proper and timely fashion and that all instruments are properly drafted and executed.

The operation of the professional corporation will be a team job. By utilizing the advice of competent professional assistance in each of the areas involved, the validity of the corporate operation will not only be established, but also the shareholder-employees will be relieved of the necessity to handle all of the administrative matters themselves. Their time will be applied, as a result, to the practice of their profession, in which capacity they can make the maximum use of their time. The operation of the corporation will require some of the time of the shareholder-employees, but wherever they can easily delegate functions to other members of the team, they will be wise to do so, because it will not only get the job done

175

better, but also it will relieve them of burdens which would otherwise take up valuable time from their rendering of the particular professional service for which they have educated and trained themselves.

8

What About Congressional Legislation and the Professional Corporation?

One of the most important aspects of professional corporations relates to congressional legislation bringing about changes in the tax law which affect professional corporations, either directly or indirectly. Legislation of this sort which affected professional corporations indirectly took place in the Tax Reform Act of 1969. Any consideration of professional incorporation must involve a careful study of the changes adopted by Congress in the Tax Reform Act of 1969 which relate to professional corporations. In addition, it has been made clear by the Treasury Department, as well as by members of Congress, including the Chairman of the Ways and Means Committee, that Congress may, and probably will, in the next few years, legislate changes in the tax law which will apply directly to professional corporations. Accordingly, any consideration of professional incorporation must give attention both to the proposals for future action by Congress, as well as to the action taken by Congress in the Tax Reform Act of 1969.

What About Congressional Legislation and the Professional Corporation?

A. What Did the Tax Reform Act of 1969 Do?

The Tax Reform Act of 1969 contains several provisions which materially affect the question of what factors should be considered in evaluating the formation of a professional corporation. Changes in the tax law brought about by the 1969 Act have affected the tax treatment of professional income in several different ways, some favorable and others to the contrary.

1. What New Problems Were Brought About?

The 1969 Tax Reform Act added three new major problems to the tax planning of professional people. These involve the new "tax preference" items of income and deductions, the new rates of tax on capital gains and a severe restriction on the use of Subchapter S "tax option" corporations.

(a) *Tax Preference Items*

A new tax, at the rate of 10% on the amount of certain "tax preference" items, to the extent that they exceed (1) $30,000 per year, plus (2) the taxpayer's income tax liability for the year, and plus (3) unused regular tax carry-over from the preceding seven years, is a problem for those with substantial tax-sheltered income and tax-sheltered deductions. It applies to the excess of investment interest over the amount of the net investment income for the year. It also applies to the amount of net capital gains, the accelerated depreciation on real property and on personal property subject to a net lease. It applies, in addition, to percentage depletion, to the extent that it exceeds the adjusted basis of the depletable property at the end of the year, as well as to some items which will ordinarily not be of importance to the professional, they being stock options, amortization of pollution control facilities and railroad rolling stock and bad debt deductions of financial institutions.

While the $30,000 figure, together with the taxpayer's taxable income for the year, will generally take care of most situations, the minimum tax of 10% on tax preference items can be a problem to the professional taxpayer who has invested heavily in real estate; for example, where interest is a large deduction item, and where capital gains, on the sale of a substantial property, may be quite large in a particular year.

(b) *Capital Gains Tax*

Under the 1969 Tax Reform Act, the deduction against ordinary income of net long-term capital losses was changed, so that each dollar of net long-term loss offsets only 50 cents of ordinary income, where the taxpayer seeks to use the offset of such net losses against ordinary income. There is still the limitation of $1,000 of ordinary income against which capital losses can be applied. While the alternative tax of 25% on long-term capital gains is kept in the law, gains in excess of $50,000 are subject to an alternative rate of 32.5% in 1971 and 35% thereafter. Accordingly, where a taxpayer has very substantial capital gains in a particular year, he can no longer count on the ceiling of 25%, if the gains exceed $50,000 in any one taxable year. This provision again hits particularly sales of real estate, since investment in real estate can often result in very substantial capital gains in one taxable year. Of course it can also apply to capital gains on other types of property; for example, gains on the sale of securities.

(c) *Subchapter S*

Until the Tax Reform Act of 1969 it was possible, as discussed in more detail in Part H of Chapter 2, for Subchapter S or "tax option" corporations, owned by less than ten shareholders, to adopt pension or profit-sharing plans, while the income of the corporation would be taxed to the shareholders as individuals. Congress, over Treasury Department opposition, decided in the Tax Reform Act of 1969 to limit the deductibilty of contributions to qualified pension and profit-sharing plans of Subchaper S corporations. This was done in much the same manner as H.R. 10 does on the self-employed. In the case of Subchapter S corporations, a "shareholder-employee" must now include in his income the contributions made by the corporation under a qualified plan on his behalf, to the extent that such contributions exceed 10% of his compensation or $2,500, whichever is less.[1] A "shareholder-employee" is an employee or officer who owns more than 5% of the stock of the corporation. The 5% also includes stock owned by his family, under the "stock attribution" rules of the Code. In addition, a qualified stock-bonus or profit-sharing plan of such a corporation must now provide that forfeitures allocable to deductible contributions may not

---

[1] Internal Revenue Code, Sec. 1379(b).

inure to the benefit of shareholder-employees to the extent that the amount forfeited is allocable to contributions previously deducted. This poses quite a problem when there are no other employees and also because the Service has not ruled on whether a Subchapter S corporation can have a stock bonus plan.[2] Payment of an excess contribution on behalf of a "shareholder-employee" of a Subchapter S corporation may be left in the tax-exempt trust. It does not, as in the case of an excess contribution to an H.R 10 plan, endanger qualification of the plan itself.

Two alternatives appear available to the owners of the Subchapter S corporation, where it runs afoul of the new Tax Reform Act limitations. One is to terminate the Subchapter S status by revoking it or transferring some of its stock. The other is to amend the retirement plan to reduce the contributions for shareholder-employees to the H.R. 10 limits.

The net effect of the change in the 1969 Act of the treatment of contributions to a qualified plan of a Subchapter S corporation has, it appears, for all practical purposes, eliminated the use of Subchapter S corporations for professionals. In other words, if a professional corporation is to be formed, then, in order to obtain the benefits of a qualified pension or profit-sharing plan, the shareholder-employees must forego the benefits of Subchapter S. They cannot now have both.

2. What Beneficial Changes Were Made?

While the Tax Reform Act of 1969 brought about certain problems for professional taxpayers, there are two provisions which were brought into the law by that Act which can prove helpful to professionals. These provisions relate to the more favorable averaging income provision and a new limitation of tax on earned income.

(a) Income Averaging

Under the 1969 Act, in order to obtain the tax benefit of income averaging, it will no longer be necessary to add to the average income for the four preceding years an amount equal to one-third of the averageable income of such years. It will only be necessary to add 20%, so that the effect will be to give greater benefits from averaging to a taxpayer whose

---

[2] Worthy, *Equality in Deferred Compensation Tax Treatment for Professionals and Others,* August 1971, Trusts and Estates, 649, at 650.

income has been gradually increasing over the years. This can be particularly helpful to a young professional in the early years of his career and also to others who run into a particularly profitable year. Capital gains will now qualify for averaging.

(b) *50% Limit on Earned Income*

Under the Tax Reform Act of 1969, a maximum marginal tax on earned income was established, this being at a rate of 60% in 1971 and 50% in 1972 and thereafter. This can be very significant to a professional taxpayer who generally will derive most of his income from earned income. Where, however, the professional has tax preference items, the benefit of the 50% limitation on earned income will be reduced. In order to determine whether the professional taxpayer loses some of the benefit of the 50% limitation, it will be necessary to see whether his tax preference items for the current year and the four preceding taxable years exceeded the $30,000 limit for tax preference items. If it proves that the taxpayer did not exceed the $30,000 limit, either in the current year or on his average of the four preceding taxable years, then he will be entitled to the benefit of the 50% limitation of tax on earned income for the year in question.

While not all professional taxpayers will need to consider all of the 1969 Tax Reform Act changes previously discussed, certainly those which apply to his particular situation will need to be evaluated, not only for the current year but for future years as well. These will, to the extent they might prove applicable, affect the overall decision as to whether the professional corporation will alleviate some of the hazards to his tax-sheltered income introduced by the 1969 Act, or whether the professional corporation will not be quite as favorable to him as it might have been previously, because he is entitled to some favorable provisions, particularly the 50% limitation on earned income, brought into the law by the Tax Reform Act of 1969.

B. What Congressional Legislation May Be Expected?

In trying to evaluate the question of formation of a professional corporation, not only will the shareholder-employees need to consider the present law under which a professional corporation would operate if organized at the present time, but also they must try to foresee, as best they can, the effect of possible future Congressional legislation which might affect the professional corporation later on. Among the subjects which have been discussed for future Congressional tax legislation will be the Treasury proposals to grant equality of treatment to partnerships and proprietorships with corporations, as far as tax-deductible retirement plans are concerned. Also involved, and part of the Treasury proposal, will be limitations on qualified plans for all corporations, or possibly for corporations whose stock is closely held. Into the picture must also be brought the various bills which have been introduced into Congress to provide for additional limitations on the handling of pension and profit-sharing funds, as well as legislation for various forms of medical aid, including the establishment of a Health Maintenance Organization.

1. What Is the Likelihood of Pension and Profit-Sharing Plans for Partnerships and Proprietorships?

The Treasury Department, speaking through its Assistant Secretary, his Deputy and the Chief Counsel of the Internal Revenue Service, has made it clear that the Department desires to introduce legislation which will permit partnerships and proprietorships to set up pension and profit-sharing plans, without the need to organize professional corporations. At the same time, however, they have attached to this proposal a qualification that a number of the limitations on pension and profit-sharing plans contained in H.R. 10 should apply to all corporations, or at least to those which are closely held.

The effect of the Treasury Department pronouncements with respect to this matter, as well as statements of members of Congress, particularly those made by the Chairman of the Ways and Means Committee, has been to discourage some professional people from forming professional corporations. Even though the Treasury Department, with the publication of T.I.R. 1019 in August, 1969, and Rev. Rul. 70-101 in March, 1970, made it clear that the Treasury Department gave its blessing to professional corporations, the numerous statements by various Treasury officials with respect to impending legislation on this subject certainly have had a dampening effect on the establishment of professional corporations during the past three years.

While everyone interested in the subject would declare himself in favor of equitable treatment for all taxpayers, whether they be professionals or not, and whether they be organized in corporate, partnership or sole proprietorship form, the accomplishment of the Treasury objectives would appear to be quite some time in the future. The problem involves consideration not only of professional corporations, but whether the same limitations that are to be imposed on professional corporations should be imposed on all corporations which have shareholder-employees. Whether there should be one rule for closely held corporations and professional corporations, on the one hand, and another rule for corporations who have many shareholders, is a matter of considerable moment, and such a differentiation between corporations would appear hard to justify.

In considering future Congressional legislation on this matter, attention must also be given to the group of senators who, in connection with the Tax Reform Act of 1969, would have imposed upon professional corporations the same contribution limitations that they imposed upon Subchapter S corporations—namely, $2,500 per year or 10% of the shareholder-employee's income—whichever is less.

(a) Are Professional Corporations Being Set Up Primarily for Tax Benefits to the Professionals?

Inherent in the Treasury proposal is the feeling that professional corporations are being established primarily to provide tax benefits for the professional shareholder-employees, rather than providing benefits for all of the employees of the professional corporation. Accordingly, the Treasury has indicated that unless the benefits are extended to partnerships and proprietorships, then the H.R. 10 limitations should be imposed upon professional corporations. On the other hand, the Treasury appears to recognize that the H.R. 10 limits are too severe and a more liberal set of rules should be adopted for all closely held corporations, including professional corporations.

(b) Limitations on Contributions

The Treasury appears to feel that the maximum compensation which should be taken into account in computing benefits or contributions to pension or profit-sharing plans should be $60,000, and the maximum rate of contribution would be limited to one-sixth of that figure, or $10,000 per year.[3] This would be four times the present H.R. 10 limit. There has been

---

[3] See footnote 2.

an indication that for aggregate-funded benefit plans, the benefits to any employee should be limited to 3%, if based on final average compensation, or 4%, if based on career average compensation. The benefits would apply to each year of service. It is possible that additional benefits or contributions might be permitted, but not through deductible contributions. With owner-employees, only service after the plan had been established could be used; whereas, prior years of service could be used in the case of non-owner employees, although perhaps prior service of owner-employees would be permitted to be taken into account in the case of plans installed within a few years after Congress passed the legislation in question. Withdrawal of contributions prior to age 59½, as in Keogh Plans, would be perhaps prohibited.

In considering the proposed limitations on contributions, it might be noted that when the proposal that finally took the form of the H.R. 10 Plan was originally proposed, it was known as the "Silverson" Plan. The Silverson proposal would have allowed a contribution limit of $10,000.[4] This limitation was eventually cut down to $2,500, with only $1,250 deductible, but later raised to $2,500 deductible. Since the Silverson Plan was first proposed in 1948, there has been a rise in dollar costs of practically 100%, due to inflation. Accordingly, the $10,000 limit first suggested in the Silverson Plan would, in today's dollars, represent considerably more than $10,000, and perhaps more like twice that amount.

(c) *Vesting*

One of the principal complaints expressed with respect to pension plans in general has been the fact that they do not vest soon enough and that employees do not have "portability" of their pensions. For this reason, it has been noted that when an employee changes jobs, there is some danger that he will lose the benefits of the retirement plan to which he has contributed for many years. This would be alleviated or eliminated by a minimum vesting requirement. The Internal Revenue Service has, during the past few years, particularly in the case of profit-sharing plans, required earlier vesting. A suggested approach on vesting would, under a "Rule of 50," require vesting of 50% of accrued benefits whenever a combination

---

4 See Silverson, *Earned Income and Ability to Pay*, 3 Tax L. Rev. 299, 315 (1948).

of age and years of service equals 50, with vesting of an additional 10% each year thereafter.

(d) *Other Keogh Plan Limitations*

Inherent in the Treasury proposals are a number of other Keogh Plan limitations, in addition to those relating to contributions and vesting. These other limitations relate to coverage, penalties for excessive contributions, distributions, choice of trustee, and exemption from Estate Tax.

As to coverage, it would seem that the general rules with respect to corporate plans, rather than the limitations of the Keogh Plan, should be used. The 70% and 80% rule of corporate plans would appear a reasonable solution. That rule has apparently worked quite satisfactorily through the years, even with small corporations.

It would seem reasonable to conclude that penalties for excessive contributions should not be as severe as they are in the case of Keogh Plans. In fact, excessive contributions probably should be handled on a carryover basis, from year to year.

The strict limitation of Keogh Plans to corporate trustees, alone, unless the plan is funded by life insurance, should be eased to permit the use of non-corporate trustees. It might be provided, however, as a precautionary measure, that there must not be a majority of shareholder trustees.

The exemption of retirement plan benefits from Estate Tax should be retained, although this preferred treatment over other items included in an estate has been questioned. It would seem there is adequate reason for Congress to provide this encouragement to private retirement plans, however, as there is for the preferred income tax treatment granted them through deductions for contributions and by tax exemption of the trust. The $5,000 death benefit should be retained as it exists for corporate plans.

All in all, it would appear that the basic concept that should govern, if there is to be unification of all retirement plans, should be that represented by the present corporate rules, which have worked so well for decades, rather than the more cumbersome and restrictive H.R. 10 rules.

(e) *Deductibility for Employee Contributions*

As an added means of expanding the coverage of private pension and profit-sharing plans, the possibility of permitting employees to make deductible contributions themselves, perhaps up to an amount of $1,000 per year, has been considered. This would be helpful to Federal government employees, who presently contribute to their own pensions. It would be helpful to other employees as well, who either contribute to their own retirement plans, or would like to do so, if a deduction were provided for their own contributions. The deductible amount should, however, probably be more than the $1,000 proposed by the Treasury. A deduction for voluntary contributions, in amounts up to $2,500 per year, with reasonable rules against early withdrawal, would seem better than the $1,000 proposed.

(f) *Other Pension and Profit-Sharing Reforms*

Many members of Congress have been seriously, and appropriately, concerned with examples of flagrant mismanagement of pension and profit-sharing funds brought to their attention. As a result, legislation to provide strict Federal supervision of such funds by Federal agencies set up for that purpose has been introduced. Hearings on such legislation have been held. It appears that improved and more strict requirements on disclosure with respect to the handling of funds will be adopted by Congress. Improved fiduciary responsibility standards will be adopted with respect to the investment of pension and profit-sharing funds and the making of loans. Whether, in the process, the entire private pension and profit-sharing system is in danger of being swept into the Social Security system, as that system continually expands, is something which will have to be considered.

The constant increase in Social Security taxes and benefits, at an ever accelerating pace, leads to the conclusion that there is a real danger that before long the entire retirement field will be virtually, or completely, pre-empted by the Federal Government. With Social Security taxes now projected at a rate which promises soon to exceed the 14% minimum income tax bracket, and with Social Security benefits constantly increasing, it seems clear that unless this trend is halted, or at least slowed down, it will not be long before private pension and profit-sharing plans will constitute merely a small superstructure, superimposed on a huge Federal Government retirement system. Whether a healthy private retirement plan system, or, for that matter, any such private system at all, is to be preserved, will pose a serious question for Congress. In the long run, all of the money that is needed to provide retirement benefits, whether they be government-administered or privately administered, must come from the profits of individual enterprise. To the extent that those profits are taken by the government, in the form of Social Security taxes, to fund the government-administered retirement system, they will not be available to the private corporations for their privately administered retirement plans.

(g) *Health Maintenance Organization*

A number of bills have been introduced in Congress to set up some form of Federal Health Maintenance Organization. This would take the place of private health and hospitalization insurance. As a part of this will be consideration of whether "denticare," in addition to medical care, should be provided by employers for their employees, or, alternatively, by the Federal government for all citizens.

The plans in Congress and by the Administration for a health maintenance organization, or an equivalent thereof in the form of a Federally funded and Federally administered program to take care of the nation's health needs, coupled with the Social Security System and a welfare program providing for a minimum income for every citizen, would lay the foundation for a comprehensive Federal program to take care of virtually all the material needs of its citizens. This would, to a large extent, supplant the private pension and profit-sharing system which we now have. Professional people would be covered by the Federal program, along with the rest of the citizens. There would be no need for professional people to set up pension and profit-sharing plans for themselves, or to provide for fringe benefits through a professional corporation. While this cataclysmic result is certainly not in the immediate offing, nevertheless, in looking down the years, it might not be too far from realization, if the present trend keeps up, by the end of the present decade.

Those who are convinced that private enterprise can do some things better than can an all-providing Federal government will wish to take a hand in providing some of these benefits through the private pension and profit-sharing system, rather than waiting for the Federal government to do it for them. A compromise between the two systems may well have to be worked out, since the pendulum seems, over the years, to swing to and fro. Accordingly, those who can see the benefits to be derived from professional corporations and the advantages of a retirement plan initiated and paid for by the owners of the enterprise, will want to give serious and active attention to this matter now, even though Congressional legislation to accomplish the same end through a government-administered program may appear to be in the offing.

2. Would Liquidation of the Professional Corporation Prove Costly?

Inherent in the Treasury proposals for unification of retirement plans is the question of whether these proposals, if adopted, will require the liquidation of the professional corporation and the retirement plans which have been adopted. Statements have been made by some Treasury officials pointing this out as a grave danger facing professional corporations. The problems, when examined carefully and objectively, would not seem quite that serious. Even if the Treasury proposals for unification are eventually enacted by Congress, so that professional people will be able, in time, to obtain retirement plan benefits without incorporating, it does not appear that many professional corporations would, in fact, choose to be liquidated.

Professional corporations have many advantages besides the tax-advantages resulting from the adoption of corporate retirement plans.[5] They provide, as many professional people have found after adopting them, a more systematic method of operating the professional enterprise. Delegation of responsibility permits more of the professionals to devote their full time to professional work, rather than having to give up valuable professional time in order to attend to business and administrative operations. These latter responsibilities, it will be found, can be assigned to employees who are primarily trained in the field of business and administration. Moreover, the time cost for their services will generally be considerably less than that of the professional himself. The experience of those who have formed professional corporations leads to the conclusion that the corporate form brings about considerably more discipline in the handling of business. It does not directly affect the handling of purely professional problems. As a result, the corporate form proves more efficient and remunerative in the long run, in terms of time, money and satisfaction.

---

[5] See footnote 1, Chapter 1.

9

What Will Be the Cost
of Incorporating?

Having considered the various factors involved in evaluating and carrying out the organization and operation of a professional corporation, one comes to the big question: What will be the cost? This involves a consideration, on the one hand, of the alternative investments that are available to a professional, through which he may accumulate property to provide for his retirement and yet obtain tax deductions without incorporating, as against the cost of incorporating and providing, through a corporate plan, the retirement plan and the "fringe" benefits that can be obtained only through incorporation. Included in this cost will be, in addition to the cost of the benefits themselves, the cost for the professional services required to bring the corporation and the retirement plan into being.

A. What Are the Alternatives?

In considering the alternatives to the professional corporation, one needs to consider the various types of investment which are available to a professional partnership, as well as to the partners as individuals. This includes the whole realm of tax-deductible investments, or, as they are sometimes labelled, "tax-sheltered" investments.

What Will Be the Cost of Incorporating?

1. What About Tax-Sheltered Investments?

The professional who has not yet formed a professional corporation has available to him a number of different categories of tax-sheltered investments. He may have been taking advantage of one or more of them. A brief review of the major types of tax-sheltered investments might well be helpful. Each of them has its own advantages and its own drawbacks. Quite often they are presented to the professional by a salesman who will stress the advantages but will neglect to bring out the pitfalls and drawbacks involved. A realistic appraisal of each of them is necessary if the professional is not to be misled by sales talk and unrealistic hopes and expectations.

(a) *Real Estate*

The most popular tax-sheltered investment for professionals, as well as for other taxpayers, certainly appears to be investment in real estate. This may take any of several different forms.

(1) Depreciable Real Estate

Real estate which is depreciable offers the opportunity for tax deductions through depreciation, as well as through payment of interest on the amounts borrowed, whether represented by mortgages or notes, as well as deductions for insurance, repairs and other expenses of operation. The types of real estate available in this category will include apartment buildings, rent houses and warehouses, as well as other types of structures. A logical investment of this type may include the structure in which the professional and his colleagues practice their profession. Within the immediate past, many professionals have taken advantage of the opportunity provided by Section 236 of the National Housing Act to invest in apartment buildings financed largely by Federal funds. Buildings occupied by solvent tenants, such as substantial business organizations, with a long-term lease, offer security, as well as definitely predictable income and, in addition, definitely predictable depreciation deductions. Many opportunities to invest in apartment buildings appear most attractive, but the projections generally are based on estimated occupancy. If the occupancy falls below the estimate, then the expected return on the investment may prove to be more illusory than real.

(2) Farms

Another popular category of real estate investment is found in the purchase and operation of a farm. Many Federal programs are available to provide deductions and income benefits, such as soil-bank programs, water-conservation programs, which provide help in building lakes, not to mention the tax deductions available through depreciation and repairs on structures and equipment used in connection with the operation of the farm. This type of investment requires a careful evaluation of the problems arising if the Internal Revenue Service determines that the farm is actually a hobby, rather than a business investment. The use of a farm as a tax shelter has been restricted by the Tax Reform Act of 1969, which sets out new rules on the recapture of farm losses, as well as the recapture of farm land expenditures. In the case of farm losses, the taxpayer is required to set up what is called an "Excess Deductions Account." This applies only to a taxpayer whose non-farm-adjusted gross income exceeds $50,000 and whose farm net loss is over $25,000. The effect of the recapture rule is to take away the benefit of ordinary deductions for farm losses in the case of taxpayers whose non-farm income exceeds $50,000 and whose farm losses also exceed the $25,000 limit. The measure effectively prevents use of a farm as a tax shelter beyond those limits. The recapture of farm land expenditures requires the recapture of deductible expenditures made for land clearance and for soil and water conservation after 1969 if farm land, held for less than ten years, is disposed of.

(3) Raw Land

A third principal category of real estate investment lies in the purchase of raw land. This offers an opportunity, in many cases, for a relatively small down payment, perhaps as little as 10% or 15% of the total purchase price. The arrangement will often provide for payments of interest only, for five years, and then payments of principal, together with interest, for the remaining five years. In the meantime, the investor can hope that, due to rising land costs, influenced in part by inflation, he will be able to sell the land at a profit, before he is required to make payments of principal, beyond the down payment of principal which was made at the time of original purchase, and a substantial part of which actually went to pay the real estate broker's commission on the original sale.

Raw land as an investment will involve a careful evaluation of the likelihood of increases in the price of the land in the vicinity and the possibility of selling the particular tract in question during the five years when interest only is to be paid. The attraction of a deduction for the interest paid each year and the sale at capital gain rates makes raw land a favored investment of many professionals. In many cases, the purchase can be arranged so that interest for the first year can be pre-paid at the time of purchase and a deduction therefor taken in that year. This type of investment, involving a large deduction each year for interest, may, however, involve the question of a "tax preference" deduction, under the Tax Reform Act of 1969, and result in imposition of the special 10% additional tax.

(b) Cattle

One of the more popular types of investment for professionals, as well as other taxpayers who find themselves in a substantial income tax bracket, has, over the years, been investment in cattle. This investment offers the opportunity for natural growth with respect to the capital investment. The investment grows in two ways, first by increase in the size of the calves and also by increase in numbers of the herd through the birth of calves. The cost of feeding and taking care of the herd can be deducted as an expense and, since the cattle are depreciable, any loss on the cattle will be deducted in full from ordinary income. The profit from the investment need not be taxed until converted into cash. Livestock used for breeding, or for draft or dairy purposes, will result in tax on the profit at capital gain rates. In the case of horses and cattle, the holding period is, however, under the 1969 Tax Reform Act, a period of 24 months, although other livestock need only be held 12 months to qualify for capital gain treatment.

Many investors in cattle have found that, in cattle as in other investments, not all that glitters is necessarily gold. Mismanagement of the investment by those charged with operating feeding operations has, to the regret of many investors, proven to be disastrous. Nevertheless, investment in cattle does have certain tax advantages and, if reliable and honest management can be secured, this type of investment can afford an opportunity for tax-sheltered investment.

(c) Equipment Leasing

Another type of tax-sheltered investment which has proven popular in the past has been that of owning and leasing equipment. In some cases, the equipment involved has been in the nature of aircraft. The investment in such cases has often proven very large in amount and, as in the case of cattle, some of the investors have found that the investment, while sound in principle, did not, in their case, work out, due to a variety of reasons, including mismanagement. Such an investment does involve the use of the depreciation deduction and, where a reliable and properly computed lease can be worked out, the investment can prove worthwhile for a group or syndicate.

(d) *Timber and Citrus Groves*

Investment in timber and citrus groves has proven popular as a tax-sheltered investment. A growth in value of the original capital is provided and the investment can later be disposed of at a capital gain rate. Sales of timber cut during the year can be taxed at capital gain rates. Hazards in connection with such investments include fire and disease. Mismanagement may also cause loss rather than profit to the investor. The Tax Reform Act of 1969 now requires capitalization of purchase, planting, cultivation, maintenance or development costs of citrus groves made in the first four years. Accordingly, all of such costs, incurred before the close of the fourth taxable year after the date of planting, will have to be capitalized. Since the trees normally start producing in the fifth year, this eliminates the tax shelter.

In areas of the country where fruit trees other than citrus are involved, some of the same opportunities, coupled with similar, if not identical problems, are likely where such an investment is considered for those engaged in the professions.

(e) *Mining*

Over the years, few investments have proven as glamorous and enticing as that of mining. In the nineteenth century, fortunes were won and lost, even before the days of income tax. For the investor, a mining investment provides the opportunity for deduction of exploration expenses, although recapture with respect to the deduction is required once production and sale of the mineral takes place. Favorable options are open to the investor at the time of recapture, he being permitted to include the amount of the previous deductions in his income from sales of the mineral and then recover the basis in his property through depletion, or forego depletion until the depletion deductions equal the exploration expenditures which he previously deducted. Unfortunately, however, investments in mining require even more careful consideration than perhaps other tax-sheltered types of investment.

(f) *Oil and Gas*

Perhaps the most talked about tax-sheltered investment is that of investment in oil and gas properties. The attraction of deducting intangible drilling expense, together with depreciation on the balance of the investment, coupled with the opportunity for depletion deductions and alternative opportunities to sell the investment itself on a capital gain basis, if successful, gives oil and gas drilling a favorable tax image. For the professional, it is possible to obtain participations in drilling syndicates sponsored by respected brokerage houses, and with sophisticated management offered. Many investors in oil and gas have found, however, that all too often their only reward is the tax benefit from charging off a dry hole. This would not be so bad if they were in a 100% bracket. Those who are fortunate enough to participate in a commercial well find, in many cases, to their regret, that more money has been lost in the oil and gas business through drilling offset wells, to delineate the producing property after a discovery well has been brought in, than has been lost in drilling wildcat wells. As a result, investment in oil and gas takes a particular type of courage and certainly warrants careful consideration of all aspects before commitment to the enterprise.

2. How Do Tax-Sheltered Investments Compare to the Tax Shelter of the Professional Corporation?

When compared with the tax shelter offered by a professional corporation, the alternative types of investment appear to present much greater hazards. In the pension or profit-sharing trust, as well as the purchase of fringe type benefits in the form of disability, health and hospitalization insurance and group life insurance, the investments above discussed which are open to a professional who does not have a professional corporation, appear far more risky than entrusting the amount of the investment to the professional management of an insurance company or a bank. This is particularly true where the funds of the retirement trust are handled by a corporate trustee or are invested in life insurance. Through the pension and profit-sharing trust, whether invested in life insurance or in securities purchased for the trust by a corporate trustee, it seems evident that while the investments through the pension and profit-sharing trust may be some-what slower in their growth and return, nevertheless they appear to offer much more safety and certainty over a long period than do the alternative investments above discussed which are available to professional people without the benefit of a professional corporation.

B. What Will the Corporate Retirement Plan Cost?

The final question with respect to implementing the decision to form a professional corporation will boil down to a question of cost. In this cost figure will be three principal categories of items; first, the cost of the various benefits, including the pension and profit-sharing plan, as well as the fringe benefits purchased through insurance, they being group life insurance, disability insurance, health and hospitalization insurance and a possible medical reimbursement plan. The second category will include the costs involved in organizing the corporation, transferring the assets from the predecessor partnership or proprietorship and setting up the books for the corporation, as well as the additional costs involved in changing the name of the entity on stationery, and in other respects. The third category of costs involves the cost of operating the corporation each year, as com-pared with the costs of operating a partnership or proprietorship.

1. What Will the Benefits Cost?

This question might best be answered in terms of the chronological sequence in which the various benefits will generally be acquired by the new corporation. At the outset, it would be desirable to acquire, as a mini-mum, the fringe benefits available through insurance, with the premiums deductible to the corporation and the benefits being free of tax to the em-ployees.

(a) *How Much Should the "Fringe" Benefits Cost?*

(1) Group Life Insurance

The cost of group life insurance will generally run approximately 1% of payroll. The amount of group life insurance would ordinarily be $50,000 on each of the shareholder-employees and commensurate amounts of coverage on other employees, depending upon the relationship of their salaries to those of the shareholder-employees. For example, if a shareholder-employee, earning $40,000 per year, would have $50,000 of group coverage, then an employee who is not a shareholder and who earns $10,-000 per year would perhaps have something like $12,500 coverage. It is not necessary that the amounts be strictly calculated, since there is no strict rule against discrimination with respect to group life insurance, although it would be well to keep the coverage within reasonable bounds. Moreover, to discriminate against non-shareholder-employees would, in the long run, from a purely selfish standpoint, be unwise public relations for the owners of the business. As noted in Part C of Chapter 6, however, if the group policy includes permanent insurance, paid up value or equivalent benefit, it must include all the employees in the same class. While $50,000 would normally be the limit on group life insurance for shareholder-employees, since that is the greatest amount that can be acquired with the premium deductible for Federal income tax purposes, where larger amounts might be desired, they could be purchased and the premiums on the coverage above $50,000 paid for by the shareholder-employees themselves.

(2) Disability Insurance

In the case of disability insurance, the cost again would be approximately 1% of payroll, although it might be slightly less. The amount of coverage can be tailored to such portion of the monthly income of the employees as may be desired by the Board of Directors of the professional corporation. For example, in the case of a shareholder-employee whose income is $40,000 per year, disability insurance to provide an income of at least one-half that amount would appear to be a reasonable objective. As in the case of group life insurance, it would be desirable to provide commensurate disability insurance coverage for all the other employees of the corporation.

(3) Medical Insurance

In the case of medical coverage, for sickness and hospitalization, the cost of such insurance would run in the area of 1.5% of payroll, with latitude to be exercised by the Board of Directors as to the type of hospital room and whether the corporation would pay for coverage of the dependents of employees, or whether the employees themselves would be given the option of paying for the coverage for their dependents, if they wished to do so, but with the corporation paying for the coverage only for the employees themselves.

(4) Medical Reimbursement Plan

The cost of a medical reimbursement plan would be more difficult to determine, with accuracy, than would be the cost of premiums to cover medical and hospital costs; but for estimation purposes, particularly in the case of a professional corporation which has a considerable number of employees, it might well be estimated that the medical reimbursement plan would cost approximately the same as would be involved in paying for premiums if the coverage were to be obtained through an insurance company, rather than through self-insurance, which is the case with a reimbursement plan without insurance protection. In the case of a professional corporation with relatively few employees, it would seem a much more conservative approach to buy the coverage through an insurance company, rather than to run the risk of self-insurance. Fortunately, however, the opportunity to decide would be in the hands of the Board of Directors. As in the case of other fringe benefits, it would be unwise to make the plan discriminatory as between different employees.

(b) *How Much Should a Profit-Sharing or Thrift Plan Cost?*

The cost of profit-sharing or thrift plan benefits is much harder to pin down than the cost of the fringe benefits just discussed. The statute provides 15% of payroll limitation on profit-sharing plans, but in many cases this would be too much to put into this one type of benefit, and certainly so at the outset. It must be remembered that the Board of Directors will wish to consider providing a pension plan as well as a profit-sharing plan, and the cost of both will need to be considered, in addition to the cost of the fringe benefits, which, as we have already noted, will aggregate approximately 3% of payroll or slightly more than that.

In addition to the question of what a profit-sharing plan would cost, there is the additional question of what type of profit-sharing plan? Should it be a plan under which the determination is made by the Board of Directors at the end of the year, or should there be some minimum fixed commitment, with latitude in the Board to add to this at the end of the year if profits permit? Another question would be whether the plan might be a thrift or savings plan, rather than a straight profit-sharing plan. In that event, the employees would make a contribution from their own income each month, ranging anywhere from 1% to 6% of their pay. Then the corporation would have the opportunity to match the employees' contributions in a ratio of anywhere from 10% to 100% of the employees' contributions, or even up to 15% of the employees' pay, if the Board so decided. In a thrift plan, only those employees who chose to make voluntary contributions would be included, although the opportunity to participate would be opened up to employees from time to time. However, there would have to be reasonable restrictions on their getting into the plan and getting out too frequently.

While the projected amount to be budgeted for the profit-sharing plan would, of course, be a matter to be decided by the particular Board of Directors in each case, a reasonable budget figure, for estimation purposes, might well be from 3 to 5% of payroll.

(c) How Much Would a Pension Plan Cost?

As in the case of profit-sharing plans, there is a great variety to choose from in selecting a pension plan. As has been discussed at length in Chapter 5, there is a large selection of pension plans and of course the cost of the plans will vary considerably. The pension plan is likely to be the most expensive benefit provided by the corporation for its employees, aside from their basic compensation and bonuses, but a reasonable estimate for the cost of the pension plan, at least for planning purposes, would be 10 to 12% of payroll. This amount, when added to the 5% for the profit-sharing plan, and approximately 3% for "fringe" benefits, would make a total of approximately 20% for all the benefits.

(d) How Will a Partner Compute the Cost of the Benefits to Himself?

The computation of the cost of the various benefits to each partner will be rather simple. Estimating the benefits at a cost of 20% of payroll, this means that each partner can plan on the package benefits costing him one-fifth of his income. If a partner has been making $50,000 per year, then he can readily determine that it will take $10,000 of his income to provide the benefits for himself, his partners and the employees of the partnership, once they become a professional corporation. At $50,000 per year, he is in a 50% income tax bracket, assuming he does not have a large number of deductions. He can readily see that approximately one-half of the benefits will be paid for through reduction in his income tax. At $50,000 per year, the reduction will not be quite 50%, since the applicable rate, once his income is reduced by the $10,000 deduction to $40,000, will be slightly less than 50%. Nevertheless, the tax savings, in broad terms, will not be difficult to compute and the 20% can be applied to whatever income is involved.

2. What Will Be the Cost of Legal, Accounting and Other Services Involved?

In addition to the cost of the various benefits to be derived from the professional corporation, there will, of course, be the cost of the legal and accounting services in setting up the corporation and in connection with the transfer of the partnership properties to the corporation, as well as setting up the books. The services of competent legal counsel and of a Certified Public Accountant will be involved. Where a fixed benefit type of pension plan is chosen, there will also be the cost of actuarial services in making the computations required to structure the fixed-benefit pension plan and provide the actuarial data required to qualify the pension plan with the Internal Revenue Service.

At the outset, it should be observed that in engaging the counsel and Certified Public Accountant, the fees for the work performed will be based on the amount of time that it takes the counsel and the Certified Public Accountant to perform their work. Since it is "professional" corporations we are discussing, there should be a clear understanding that when a person engages competent professional help on a problem, the help they provide will be worth what it costs. If not, then a bad choice has been made in selecting counsel and the accountant. It will be shortsighted economy to try to drive too hard a bargain with counsel and with the accountant, as it would be to try to bargain too hard with a surgeon who is undertaking to perform an intricate operation. The best help available is, in the long run, likely to be the least expensive.

(a) *What Will the Legal Services Cost?*

The legal services involved will fall into two categories. The first is involved in the organization of the corporation itself. Under the tax law, legal fees for organizing corporations are deductible over a five-year period.[1]

---

[1] Internal Revenue Code, Sec. 248.

What Will Be the Cost of Incorporating?

The recommended fee schedules of the various state bar associations will generally provide that legal fees for organizing a corporation should run somewhere in the vicinity of $300 to $500. In addition, there will be the filing fees with the Secretary of State and the cost of a minute book and corporate seal. Also involved may be some out-of-pocket disbursements for long-distance telephone calls to the Secretary of State and cost of printing the stock certificates.

The balance of the legal services involved in connection with the organization of a professional corporation and the transfer of properties to it, as well as the various instruments involved, will be in the nature of deductible expenses. For a corporation on a cash basis of accounting, these fees will be deductible in the year in which paid. A considerable number of legal instruments, in addition to the Articles of Incorporation and the By-laws, which instruments would be included in the cost of legal fees for the organization of the corporation, will be involved. The preparation of the compensation agreements for the shareholder-employees requires careful drafting and will undoubtedly involve conferences between legal counsel and the shareholders of the corporation. The stock purchase agreement will need to be carefully drafted and discussed, as will the preparation of the pension and profit-sharing plans. In addition, the pension and profit-sharing plans will need to be qualified with the Internal Revenue Service and this requires the filling out and marshalling of data for the Internal Revenue Service forms. The transfer of the properties from the predecessor partnership or proprietorship to the corporation will involve a number of legal instruments, including consideration of leases, as well as transferring the title to property to the corporation. There will be problems involved in the question of when the partnership should be terminated and what assets of the partnership should be left in the partnership, what might be transferred to a separate corporation for the purpose of owning the property (and perhaps leasing it to the professional corporation) and what items should, in fact, be transferred to the professional corporation itself.

In connection with the adoption of the pension and profit-sharing plan, careful consideration will need to be given to the question of whether a master plan might save legal and accounting fees. This must be compared with the sacrifice of flexibility in the plan and a narrowing down of the options available to the shareholder-employees in preparation of the plan.

What Will Be the Cost of Incorporating?

It should be kept in mind that setting up a professional corporation involves a large element of estate planning for each of the shareholder-employees, since the professional corporation plays a large role in the overall estate plan of each individual involved. Consequently, the ideal solution will involve a careful analysis of how the professional corporation fits into the estate plan of each shareholder-employee.

Lawyers find that their clients quite often are seeking a rule of thumb as to what the legal and accounting fees might be. This poses a difficult judgment problem. In the case of the one-man corporation, the legal and accounting fees will, of course, be less than where there are several shareholders. Each additional shareholder-employee will add to the cost. One might well ask, "Why should this be?" The answer lies in the fact that if the work is to be done properly, it is essential that the plan fit not just one shareholder-employee. It must fit all of them. They all have varying estate and tax problems, as well as different cash needs. They may have differing investment goals. One shareholder may have a large family; another may be single. The problems of the older shareholder will be quite different from those of the younger. The work may very well involve separate conferences with each shareholder-employee. In such conferences, his accountant should definitely be involved, and perhaps his life underwriter, and even the shareholder's wife as well.

(b) How Much Should the Accountant's Fees Be?

To handle the setting up of the books of the corporation, preparing tax returns of the predecessor partnership, the corporation and the shareholder-employees, will involve considerable work for the accountant. Again the shareholder will want a rule of thumb. The accountant, when he has reviewed all the facts, may very well, in a given case, estimate what his fees will run. It must be borne in mind that the accountant, as in the case of the lawyer, may well have to have individual conferences with each shareholder-employee and their wives, in addition to those he has with the group jointly.

Where a fixed benefit pension plan is involved, there will be actuarial responsibilities which will require the payment of actuarial fees. These will generally be based on time cost. As a rule, a fixed benefit plan will generally not be adopted unless there are three or more shareholder-employees, since a money purchase type pension plan will ordinarily be more satisfactory for the one- or two-man corporations. The actuarial fees again will be less for the smaller professional corporation and will move up as the number of shareholder-employees involved increases. With the larger group, the actuarial computations and projections will be greater and the likelihood of individual conferences, either in the actuary's office or on the telephone, will increase as the number of shareholders increases.

In looking at the total fees involved, one might be tempted to throw up his hands and say, "Whatever it is, that is too much." When, however, the total fees for professional services involved are compared with the total contributions that are going to be made to the pension and profit-sharing plan over a period of years, and with the growth in value of the trust funds, the fees are not likely to prove large. It should be borne in mind also that the fees are deductible and the net cost to the taxpayer in a 50% bracket is only one-half of the total. The job of setting up a professional corporation is not too involved as a matter of principle, but it does need to be done properly, if it is to be done at all. It involves, in addition to forming the corporate organization, transferring the properties and drafting the instruments, as well as setting up the books. There is need for able legal counsel, and the role of the Certified Public Accountant should not be minimized. The matter is one which requires a competent professional team. No one of them can do the entire job alone. They must work as a team.

In addition to the legal and accounting fees involved, it must be noted that there will be a small amount of other expenses involved in the organization of the professional corporation and transfer of the property. The change of name of the organization will call for the printing of new letterheads, fee statements and there will be some additional costs for other expenses incidental to the change of the name of the entity and the transfer of property involved.

3. What Will Be the Additional Costs Involved in Operating the Corporation?

The corporation will experience some costs in operation from year to year which have not been involved in operating the predecessor partnership. In each state there will be a franchise tax to pay each year and there may be a slight income tax as well, payable to the state. Each of these will require the preparation of tax returns. In addition, as noted in Chapter 1, the Social Security and unemployment taxes will be slightly greater. The same applies to the additional workmen's compensation costs. As far as the year-to-year costs are concerned, it may well be that the entity will spend somewhat more on accountants' fees than in the case of the partnership. In return for that, however, the benefits of a more businesslike operation are likely to more than offset the additional accounting cost. The keeping of minutes and other corporate records, as well as holding of shareholders', directors' and executive committee meetings, as well as minutes in connection therewith, may involve some additional legal fees each year, as well as the expenditure of some time on the part of the shareholder-employees, but again the reward, in terms of more efficient operation of the entity from a business, tax and financial standpoint, is likely to more than offset the additional expenditures of money and time involved.

It would be hard to estimate any precise figure for additional legal and accounting costs, since each case will vary so considerably, depending upon the availability of many of these services from present personnel. In the case of a medical clinic, the value of a competent clinic manager can hardly be overestimated. The increase in use of para-professionals will enable the professional corporation to take care of many of these services by the utilization of its own staff, with resort to outside counsel and accounting help mainly on a consulting or check-up basis.

The experience of many professional groups already proves that the adoption of the professional corporation form will often bring about the institution of more efficient procedures in the overall operation of the entity. Practices which were expensive in terms of time costs, waste and careless attention to bookkeeping and other details, can often be brought into line. The organization of the corporation provides the occasion and the opportunity, if seized upon by the shareholder-employees, to streamline the organization and perhaps get more profit from the same amount of aggregate fees. Collection procedures can often be improved and in many medical clinics, which have in the past few years changed from partnership to association form, it has proven possible, by setting goals for performance and delineating objectives more clearly, as well as furnishing targets and standards for performance, to increase the overall productivity of the clinic and thus offset, to a substantial extent, the cost of the pension, profit-sharing and fringe benefit programs, without reducing the take-home pay of the doctors. This will certainly not automatically follow from the organization of the professional corporation, but the opportunity for improving the operation of the professional group, or at least the opportunity for a check-up on its operation, may well be provided by the study that is involved when going into the professional corporation and the highlighting of all the factors involved, including the compensation basis, as well as the bonus plan, for the shareholder-employees.

The professional corporation is certainly not a panacea and should not be regarded as such. It is a new, and can often prove to be a very helpful, tool which, if properly used, can help the professional to obtain more for himself, his family and for the non-professional employees of the organization, than might have been possible in the predecessor partnership or proprietorship. Whether it will prove to be such depends on many circumstances, not the least of which is the care and attention that the shareholder-employees devote to the matter themselves. If they will take the time to make sure that they have reviewed all of the factors involved, have a good understanding of them and then make a careful and deliberate decision, there is a good prospect that, as they look back on the steps a number of years later, as have some associations done who made the decision a number of years ago, they are likely to figure that "the game was worth the candle."

INDEX

Index

Index

Index

Index

Index

Index

Index

Index